Fruits of Eden, Herbalism and the Occult

FRUITS
Herbalism

TARL WARWICK
2015

Fruits of Eden, Herbalism and the Occult

This text and all of the illustrations included herein are the sole copyright of the author. In no way may this work be edited, duplicated, sold, distributed, altered, or copied without the express written consent of the author, whether in printed, electronic, chemical, or any other form.

Passages from this text may be quoted, analyzed, or used in accordance with fair use policies under US law. The author is easily contacted online with a cursory search of the internet for those who want permission to use more of the text for various purposes (with attribution.)

Fruits of Eden, Herbalism and the Occult

Teaching the art of identifying, using, cultivating, and understanding the value of botany with regards to the occult.

DISCLAIMER:

The author does not condone the ingestion of toxic or illegal substances which may be listed within this text- all information provided within this book is provided for educational reasons only, and should not be construed as condoning or promoting the use of mind altering, toxic, or illegal substances. The reader assumes all risk upon using any information taken from this text within any form of ritual. This book should not be construed as a guidebook for the ingestion of any substance listed.

Fruits of Eden, Herbalism and the Occult

INTRODUCTION

To the occultist, almost nothing is more useful than a working knowledge of the botanical world. It doesn't seem to matter what variety of mysticism is being practiced, what culture it comes from, what materials it makes use of in its work; herbalism is innate to virtually all occult traditions, regardless of origin, connecting them all, in its own natural way. If we look to the Hermetic tradition, indeed, and if the concept of *as above so below* holds any veracity at all, we would expect the cosmic to be reflected totally and completely in the natural.

Throughout all the world, in every tradition, plants have been used in some way as part of magickal rites- for flavoring incense, making candles, consecration rituals, curses, prayers and invocations, purifying or destroying. Indeed, a well stocked garden (and the knowledge to use it) was, in the middle ages, often seen as evidence that an individual was a practicing witch. This unfortunate individual was, depending on the area, was either a highly valued member of society or else beheaded or burned at the stake.

The early identification of those with herbal knowledge as at least *de facto* witches is not surprising- for in ancient times, the use of a psychedelic or of herbal medicine was unknown to most of the population and handled by a few individuals who could grow and care for important plants, some of which were used to disastrous ends (such as Alexander's unfortunate succumbing to hellebore, if tales are true.)

In the middle ages, when knowledge was largely lost on the illiterate population, only the monks and the witches had any sort of real medical skills. The ability to cure sickness through herbalism was indeed seen as miraculous (or horrifically scary) by passers-by who thought that parsley was the devil's plant with roots that seeped into the cavernous halls of hell. The type of superstitions imagined by the christian laity and clergy roughly mimic their treatment of creatures encountered in the new world; as monstrous.

Fruits of Eden, Herbalism and the Occult

It is for these and other reasons that plants are inseparable from the occult- even the notion of a natural surrounding for ritual use (in nature itself that is) seems more often to appeal to the occult than a bleak cityscape bereft of all life. To meditate within a cave can be seen as more authentic, more productive, than doing it in an apartment. Small wonder that tales of the same appear in virtually all ancient cultures, from the primitive copper age through the bronze and into the period of high antiquity, continuing thereafter.

When I set out to write this book, I at first planned primarily to stick to classifying plants relevant to the occult topic, in an encyclopedic manner. Upon further consideration, I realized two things:

Firstly, that there are already a large number of books on the topic, and that there would, if I wrote in that manner, be no real way in which it would distinguish itself from any other dozen randomly chosen books on the topic. A simple encyclopedia of herbal species of note within the occult would not specifically be of value to anyone at this stage in the occult.

Secondly, that beyond merely listing relevant plants, there is a great deal of material related to the topic that has not been put in many (sometimes any) other books on occult botany. What herbal text has designated peripheral topics as important, such as the creation of charcoal, which is so closely paired with herbalism both in its use as a stratum for incense as well as its properties when added to soil?

Thus, I decided to include basic plans and gardening techniques, the manner of making incense, and certain incense and candle recipes which can be manufactured by those who wish to pursue such things- not only is this helpful to the occultist, but they are in themselves valuable skills anyways which can be capitalized upon. Even the manner of making charcoal which can be used for incense or for enriching soil is seemingly lost on most occultists. I additionally decided to add some information about the historical context of most of these plants- fusing a scientific with a spiritual approach. This may be seen by some fringe occultists as unnecessary or even heretical- so be it, science and spirituality are the same, as even early philosophical works suggest. The public's morbid fascination with grimoires containing little more than curse after curse designed after the will of sometimes misconstrued or imaginary demonic forces is a christian invention only, and some occultists merely play along.

Even those who do not possess land to cultivate can always grow some of these plants indoors- the effort involved is actually fairly minimal as long as a person does not forget their plants until the soil resembles the Mojave desert- tales of growing things being as difficult as Atlas holding up the planet are largely overblown and the result of urban individuals thinking that it requires no physical effort and watching as their chemically-sprayed crops wither. It is also important to stress the need for organic gardening whenever these herbs are for use in incense or to be consumed ritualistically. While plants remain "technically" edible after heavy pesticide spraying, this should be discouraged, as many occult paths require a reverence for and closeness with nature to begin with. "Natural is best" ought to be the operating ethic behind occult gardening and herbalism.

I have spent many years as an occultist, but I have spent far more years growing things- the process of constructing a small, simplistic area to raise plants for ritual reasons is not difficult, and requires four parts knowledge to one part actual work. Through understanding the content of this work, it will be easy for any occultist to succeed in their own experimentation with cultivating life forms for ritual use, or for their own deified amusement.

There is one brief final point here- that raising life is itself a godlike behavior- as understood by the Persians, in whose culture the nobility alone was allowed to care for ornate fields of plants, because they realized that control of lower life forms was intrinsically deified. From seed to seeding, this cultivation controls every aspect of the entire life of another living thing.

Fruits of Eden, Herbalism and the Occult

TABLE OF CONTENTS

I
The historical impact of occult herbalism (p. 8-19)

II
An encyclopedic list of some plants used to retain health and protect (p. 20-92)

III
An encyclopedic list of some plants used for working curses and necromancy (p. 93-112)

IV
An encyclopedic list of some mind altering plants (p. 113-144)

V
An encyclopedic list of plants used in love and lust spells (p. 145-168)

VI
Building and maintaining a small garden (p. 169-180)

VII
VII: Making charcoal and its uses (p. 181-194)

VIII
Making incense, paper, ink, and smudges naturally (p. 195-211)

IX
X: Finding or creating an outdoor, natural ritual space (p. 212-222)

X
A running index of occult-related plants and their uses (p.220-239)

CHAPTER ONE
The History of Occult Herbalism

To most modern-day occultists, herbalism and botany are peripheral at best to their mystic experience- relegated primarily to the scent of incense, or else decoration around their altar.

To ignore the historical impact of botany (and related soil and geological sciences) is to imply that occultism has no similarity to science, something which seems odd given the traditional visage of a bearded, robed alchemist surrounded by charts, maps, and instruments, upon whose table sits ancient leather bound volumes of herbal and geological lore, both of his own design and that of others. Upon this same table, whether we regard authentic occultism or Hollywood-infused quasi-witchery circa the silver screen era, we might expect to see a bundle of wolfsbane, some hanging garlic bulbs to torment demons or ward off vampires, perhaps with a bowl of powdered herbs used to exorcise the devil or bring forth some abomination from the abyssal void beyond the veil of reality.

In fact, there are many sciences which are intertwined with the occult- something which scientists of the modern age forget, considering, for example, alchemy as detached somehow from chemistry, despite the roots and origins of their trade being forged by ancient scholars and clerics who dabbled with strange chemical brews, sometimes in an effort to create gold, and sometimes in medicinal efforts. That alchemists did not create actual gold by boiling chunks of bark in mercury is clear, but the basic idea, to classify and arrange matter into a hierarchy modeled loosely after cosmic ideas took hold. Today, the laboratory of the alchemist is perhaps more sophisticated, but no less confusing (and occult!) to the laypeople.

Herbalism, in both an occult and non-occult sense, is perhaps one of the oldest human endeavors, from the origins of agriculture

Fruits of Eden, Herbalism and the Occult

among ancient city states and tribes, to the propagation of herbs for medicine (and associated medicinal rituals) to of course the ever present midwives who could easily induce abortion if they knew which plants or substances were capable of inducing them. In the middle ages, if you were shot in the arm with an arrow, and your wound festered, you almost surely lost the limb if you didn't visit the local wise woman with her bags of herbs, who knew that a little powdered sulfur, rock salt, and chamomile, would draw the infection right out and destroy any microbes present there. If you visited what was then considered a "modern" medical mind, amputation was the likely course.

Even in the lauded tomes of knowledge passed down from Greece and Rome we have numerous references to botany- and the astute observer will notice that tribes which today have differed little from their primary incarnations during the prehistoric age, have a working knowledge of plant toxins and botanical medicine, indicating a strong likelihood that the shamanistic rituals and hunting knowledge they use predates written records, perhaps going even further back beyond the scope of modern *homo sapiens*. This is not surprising, given that, whatever climate man inhabited, he encountered plants which were toxic, plants which were edible, and plants which served other, more ritualistic purposes. The process of identifying edible species alone was a matter of life and death for the hunter gatherers of the early era of man, although we might imagine that the similarity of mythic traditions among widely disparate classes of humans in early antiquity could be evidence that some sort of pre-diaspora group was at least using what would be classed as horticulturalist methodology before even the last ice age; this rabbit hole goes so deep that it will require, I imagine, its own book.

We can find within the occult several trappings which seem almost universal, and we can plainly see the usefulness of herbal knowledge when we observe them.

Firstly, the presence of incense- which prior to the creation of synthetic, inorganic scent compounds, was made entirely using extracted compounds from certain plants.

    Secondly, the presence of special, ritualistic cloths for altars, and for clothing, which would largely have been made from plant based materials except where they were made from animal skins (which still would likely have been treated, in some regions, with tannins from boiling acorns or other plant materials!) Even in the latter case, the animals raised for slaughter were themselves fed plant life to survive- even in the christian bible we have the strange tale of changing the appearance of goats using striped wooden rods which were supposedly placed before them while they ate- an occult ritual not considered occult, I suppose, by the Abrahamists.

    Thirdly, the common presence of a wand, scepter, or rod- a common feature of rituals, and an even more common feature of the archetypal wizard, wise man, or magically inclined sage- as being useful for rituals, as well as for indicating that "this is a wise individual which should not be harassed." Even the superstitious silver screen generation likens a wand to the presence of magick. That this simplistic instrument was merely a director for the occult energy made or used, or else a mere symbol of penile potency paired with the cup representing the feminine aspect of magick, doesn't really matter considering its all encompassing presence in both actual occultism and that which is fake but treated as real in the media or entertainment industries.

    Fourthly, the presence of fire- which would most often have been made using special wood or charcoal of a fragrant nature (cedar, hickory, etc) which would further have created a ritual space. In ancient times merely boiling water was probably considered a form of magick.

    In fact, other than metal or stone implements, most trappings of any ritual whether modern or ancient revolve directly or indirectly around the use of plants- something which is also a common feature to architecture, engineering, and other fields of study.

    In the medieval era, as mentioned in the introduction, a

Fruits of Eden, Herbalism and the Occult

knowledge of herbal lore was often seen as a dangerous sign that the wise individual was practicing some sort of evil mystic system, rendering them capable of poisoning wells or killing off the wheat crop right before harvest. That the lives of individuals who claimed witchery to explain their ills were made far worse by their killing off of some of the more intelligent people of the time period, while the kings court often had at least one alchemist constantly endeavoring to make gold out of lead (and subsequently discovering other, more realistic chemical properties, sometimes with an eye to herbalism,) Is fairly clear. A community without its midwife was a sad community indeed, and these actions likely prolonged the dark ages, just as the systematic slaughter of cats (also a potent occult facet, especially in Egyptian lore) prolonged and exacerbated the plague and probably was indirectly responsible for the wiping out of up to a third of the European population via the fabled miasmas, which seemed to emerge from the fringes of each village only to leave it in ruins.

The occult and science are in fact often the same thing, with the exception of purely spiritual concepts such as, say, invoking demons or divine forces- most of the behaviors associated with a witch in the middle ages would today be seen as concerned more with earth science than the occult. However, the occult world of today has partially lost its potency with regards to the natural sciences in favor of ever more fanatic rituals which don't involve any working knowledge of botany. These days, many occultists are solely concerned with buying collectible grimoires, which are sometimes merely adaptations of older ones such as the *Grimoirium Verum*.

In fact, one disturbing trend of the modern occult movement (which some argue is in a renaissance period due to its fantastically high growth rate in the wake of the internet age) is an almost combative attitude towards occultists practicing herbalism, as "not authentic" or "not occult enough" but these condemnations seem based more on the connection between "inauthentic" pagan paths with nature, than on nature itself being inauthentic. I have heard more than one supposed magi label those working with roots and leaves as merely "fluff bunny" (as the colloquial term goes) magicians of little power or value. Oddly enough, these same rootworking paleo-occultists as we might term them have a vast arsenal of toxic compounds derived from the plant and mineral worlds fully capable of wiping out thousands of people in a single go. There is a reason why some of the most crippling chemical weapons ever deployed by modern militaries in their occasional fit of genocide are derived from plants (ricin) or from anaerobic decomposition processes involving organic materials. (botulism.)

But truly, what would the court alchemist be without his garden? Would the shaman not need a well stocked table full of hallucinogenics to enter into a spiritual trance? The Siberians ingest *amanita* mushrooms in an attempt to commune with their divine forces- and these rituals are some of the oldest (some would say progenitor) forces behind occultism. There is a certain enormous wooden statue from the Mesolithic period found buried in a bog in Russia called the *Shigir Idol* which to me is nothing more or less than evidence of fairly sophisticated crafting abilities in the hallucinogenic-imbibing tribes of the steppe and taiga of that same time period there.

Had a half witted caveman not stumbled upon a patch of psychedelic plants and eaten them, would he have understood even the most basic rudiments of the mystic way? The use of botany in our day to day lives is so prevalent that the entirety of civilized culture would crash into a heap of rubble and ash were nobody to understand such methodologies. Oddly, were one herbalist to survive such a societal and physical collapse, they may very well find a great many uses for those same ashes, where material science overlaps herbalism.

The modern occult movement seems to have been partially tainted by a reliance upon technology- the same technology that makes it possible for a person in Kenya to read and understand a 200 year old manuscript written in Germany and scanned into *pdf* format by someone who is living in Nepal has also forced many occultists (who live in urban areas largely bereft of nature) to seek guidance and knowledge that in turn is largely developed by urbanites in a similar situation. Oddly enough this is roughly similar to the abandonment of volkische, tribalistic religious and spiritual systems during the period of high antiquity, when urbanization under Roman provincial systems began to dominate the Mediterranean region. I try to look for synchronicity where it exists and there is a massive synchronicity (itself an intrinsic occult concept) between the current era, in some ways, and antiquity. This time, Rome is the Western sphere entirely; far more massive, possessed of nuclear weapons, and which may prevail on that basis alone because its toppling will bring about armageddon.

There is nothing wrong, per se, with this sort of modernized *techno-occultism* but like with any force within the spiritual realm it has strengths, but also weaknesses. A large amount of weight has been given to mystic traditions which do not require a breadth of herbal knowledge, precisely because as the world becomes more urbanized, more crowded, and more artificial, it becomes harder for the occultist to even encounter nature without going many miles out of their way. Even most land that isn't covered by cities is covered by agricultural sprawl, unless the magician wishes to travel to the desert or high into the mountains- areas which might be far removed from them. I myself have been blessed to reside in an area which is primarily forested, because there are too many mountains for land development to be financially feasible.

However, there can be a peaceful coexistence between the technologically adept but naturally disinclined modern occult movement, and their more agrarian counterparts- through an interchange of ideas between these two forces, which amusingly mimic the difference between urban and rural occultism in any time period. This concept, that of *urban magick* and *rural magick* is mirrored in the interplay between mainstream religious and spiritual forces, and folkloric counterparts which tend to predate them. We see this in the tourist-driven modern "voodoo" movement in New Orleans shadowed by the various cajun and creole spiritual forces in outlying areas which remain more natural and more intact. The former is driven by money, the latter by actual belief.

Fruits of Eden, Herbalism and the Occult

And here is another revelation- this interplay between the urbanized and ruralist occult schools is not new, but merely new in regards to the technology available to interchange ideas- for even the word used by the ancients to describe the rural population was "paganus" or the modern "pagan" to describe uncouth mountain and meadow dwelling tribes who had little or no access to substantial urban areas. Uncouth, I say, in mannerisms, for the Romans loved to adopt their regional deities and practices and absorb them anyways.

And the pagan tribes, of course, were marked by the use of herbalism and asymmetric-style occultism, which revolved heavily around dance, music, and the ingestion of mind altering substances, in direct opposition to the priests of the Roman gods in cities, which saw all of the above as things to be regulated and have laws built around, such that the major difference between a ritualistic, deity-inspired Roman parade in Rome and the dancing and marching of the pagans in the outer realm of the empire, would not have been in form so much as in function. Literally, the out-lands were full of people who believed the idea of spiritually-related taxation was nonsensical. The urban Romans, who loved bureaucracy and paperwork, saw little problem with it.

The first notable texts about herbalism were, not surprisingly, called herbals, written to document, largely, the medicinal use of various plants which were endemic to whatever region the author decided was appropriate (and often the one they hailed from.) These tomes of knowledge were among the most scientific volumes written during the dark ages- and yet, despite being so advanced in thought, their authors largely mixed them with astronomical, astrological, and metaphysical lore (plants being "of certain planets" or important for certain spiritual events.) They number in the hundreds, scattered across antiquity into the Medieval and Renaissance eras and explode in popularity around the time of the enlightenment. We even have an extant *Apicius* from the fourth century- a Roman cookbook with all of its own culinary herbal uses.

Fruits of Eden, Herbalism and the Occult

In the modern age, science thus frowns upon such works, giving them the cold shoulder not because they contained errors but because they were too involved with the spiritual world- something western science now shuns- which is strange, because were it not for early herbal pioneers, many of the synthetic drugs now used within the pharmaceutical industry would not exist- for they are based upon chemicals derived from plants (and in some cases, plants are still the primary or sole source of such chemicals.) Quinine, Aspirin, early sulfa drugs, Penicillin derived from fungus, and so forth.

Indeed, recently certain African nations have been begging for certain herbal medicines which combat malaria, realizing that the western supply of synthetics is not inherently superior to the herbal remedies, and that the synthetic supply is losing its effectiveness over time. These natural sources are renewable and cheap as well. At the same time they also clamor to produce and buy the infamous DDT, a synthetic material, to destroy mosquitoes at their sources.

The same holds true for the occult- the modern techno-mage is faced with an interesting dilemma, in which he or she realizes that a pdf file and a laptop computer are not providing the sense of *connectedness* with the spiritual realm that they so desire- that in order to access this frame of mind, they need to metaphorically head for the sacred groves for a more authentic experience. The current occult renaissance has been a long time in the making, and has taken several steps along the way into its current incarnation- and herbalism has been right along for the ride, slowly re-establishing its supremacy as one of the more major occult fields.

The establishment of this age of mystic awareness can be traced directly to the mid 1960s and the rise of the flower children and hippie movement. If it were not for the drug using hippies who headed off into the woods to run around naked, our western culture would still be largely a legalistic christian culture as it was prior to the advent of psychedelic rock and the common usage of LSD (a partially synthetic

Fruits of Eden, Herbalism and the Occult

fungus compound) and various plants from deserts and forests which all led them to turn on to the music and tune in to the strange vibrations.

These anti cultural rebels experimented frequently with all forms of occultism- both new age and authentic, all across the western world during this period- and anyone who has seen video taken from Woodstock knows that more than a few "magical" herbs were in use there. Crystals, Ouija boards, tarot cards, and books about every imaginable mystic system littered the stores of large cities (particularly on the west coast) for an entire generation (my parent's generation) to consume.

In the 1970s, it remained much the same- although a rising crowd of liberal christians were repeatedly frightened by Hollywood's lurid tales such as *The Exorcist* which convinced them that dabbling in even childish occultism could cause them to be possessed by Satan. Where earlier stock horror had titillated a willing audience, it now chilled them to the bone.

I can still remember being a child and my mother having crystals hung around our apartment (which of course contained a large number of things painted in the typical psychedelic colors of the 1970s.) And it wasn't until the mid 1990s that the hippie fever had essentially died down. At this slightly later period, I remember the end of the *Satanic Panic* and parents giving certain totemic-style amulets to their children to ward off evil forces. I myself had a "witch wood" pendant (I'm still not sure where this tradition stems from) which I unfortunately lost at some point and used to carry a quartz crystal in my pocket at all times to bring luck.

The occultism of the 1960s and into the 1970s was, however, partially tainted by fears of cults and drug use gone wrong, and by the 1980s a new counter-counterculture of white, middle class yuppies had arisen, intent upon doing everything possible to demonize the use of any mind altering substance, and surely, of any occult system.

Fruits of Eden, Herbalism and the Occult

From that point forward, swore the straight-laced squares, there would be no more witchery in the west- everything would go back to normal: ice cream and apple pie would abound in this retro 1950s land. It seemed that they were winning, as well- by the late 1980s, occultism had largely gone underground (with the exception of Wicca, which had managed to escape too much harassment from the mega church televangelists because the Wiccans managed to convince the jaded christians that they had a common enemy in devil worshipers.) Perhaps this is why the more "dark" elements of the occult consider the largely white-magick practicing Wiccans to be enemies- a sort of treason in an era where christians ran roughshod even over secular legal systems in their persecution of "the devil worshipers."

However, something then happened that the "moral majority" did not intend.

In the waning hours of the 1980s, into the 1990s, the rise of the technocratic post-yuppie underclass had all but doomed the moral majority with their gold plated mega churches. The internet, slowly rising in power, and slowly becoming more affordable to the middle class, soon allowed individuals outside of the mainstream to tell their own story, free from the censorship of mainstream publishers, and free from the ever present hawkishness of the all-too-gullible press. Soon, chat rooms and forums developed, allowing even the most fringe elements of any developed nation to prosper and win the hearts and minds of captive audiences.

And herbalism was right there.

It wasn't very long until hordes of Satanists, Wiccans, Pagans, and general occultists the world over congregated online to discuss their content with one another, including enough herbal lore to stock a large library. Sites developed which catered to ever more specific audiences, until someone researching herbalism, and someone researching psychoactive plants, could both find, on the same site or

Fruits of Eden, Herbalism and the Occult

different sites, enough information to allow them hours or days of study. The diminution of each separate or differentiated occult system began, as they were broken down into ever more concentrated circles, allowing someone doing research into any of them to never exhaust the material thereof. Even at this very moment, I imagine that hundreds of texts are being translated for the first time, whether into English or some other language. The wealth of knowledge now present in electronic form is absolutely off the rails.

In fact, the naturist path of most occultism has had a predominantly mutualistic relationship with the age of technology since this time period- occultism increased on the internet and in popular culture partially because of the wide scope of material available from older works, and in turn this increase led to newer works, and the availability of fringe material. This seems to have also been the case with paranormal research, and alternate religions as well. When I was a child, in the 1990s, the paranormal began to gain popularity on television with fictional series, then morphed into the first few quasi-documentary style movies and series on the topic (a direct evolution from the days of Nimoy on *In Search Of...*

Thanks to computer technology, texts from ancient times are no longer relegated to large urban libraries and the back shelves of rare book shops- waves of ever older and ever more hard to find materials are finding their way into the online world- and many of us have attempted to speed up this process through scanning materials to pdf form which were not formerly available, increasing the collective occult library of the computer age exponentially. Additionally, in this age of technology, ancient relics are being found once again with the same vigor once associated only with the Victorian era in which mummies were being dug out of crypts to powder and sell as medicine or to burn as fuel. The mainstream appears to have tried and failed to all but ignore this massive expansion of occult lore and ritual.

Unfortunately, this technology has been more limited in form at accounting for herbalism and the herbal occult- you can find literally

Fruits of Eden, Herbalism and the Occult

tens of thousands of guides and scans online which deal with summoning demons, but relatively few comprehensive guides for the classification and use of occult herbalism- and even fewer manuals which contain historical context or how-to guides for those who want to propagate their own garden of magical delight. Therefore, it is up to modern occultists to study the topic and produce new material; the occult is not static, it is not stagnant, and must never be so.

Partially, the situation seems to have arisen from the fact that most good collections of herbal knowledge on the internet are paired with internet stores, where the people providing information on using such plants are also the ones selling them- why would they endanger their sales by telling people how to grow such things? Further, while a great many herbals exist, many are in Italian, Latin, and Greek. Those who would translate such works are too busy working on other historically important works, it seems.

In any case, however, the occult renaissance has led to an ever greater interest in herbs and herbalism- and amusingly, some of these groups which spring up are at least partially environmentalist (sometimes blatantly so) in form, specifically admonishing members to make use of, and protect, the natural world around them. Let us now remember that Nostradamus himself- regardless of whether you consider him a prophet- began as a plague doctor who sold pills made with rose hips. His effective dealings with pestilence were largely rooted in his adaptation of the idea of running water being cleansing. He was right, for the wrong reasons; for he was actually blasting acres of filth out of the ground and aging sewer systems and creating an early form of mass sanitation. Surely, his herbal knowledge was of help in this considering the antimicrobial properties of many plants with which he attempted to destroy miasmas.

A city may crumble into the Earth, but the mountain next to it may stand for millions of years- the power of nature is unchallenged and unswayed and shall always remain as such.

CHAPTER TWO
Plants grown or used to retain health and to protect

ALOE
(Aloe Vera)

Aloe Vera is one of the most easily potted and easily grown (and effective) medicinal plants on Earth. A long lived succulent, it may grow to enormous sizes, and its fleshy leaves contain a slimy substance that almost immediately soothes and begins to heal burns.

Mentioned as early as ancient Egyptian times for its health benefits, Aloe is also sometimes used as a food (although some claim it is mildly carcinogenic) and obviously as a low-care houseplant. In southern climates, it can be naturalized to an outdoor setting. In a Northern climate, somewhere cold, it must remain indoors.

Aloe is not so much known for its use in ceremonial rituals as it is known for its use in folk medicine with an occult twist- its usefulness in treating burns is undeniable (for which it may be kept on hand for those who practice pyromancy, or who intend to hold a ceremonial bonfire or burn sigils.) Long used in Ayurveda, it actually functions as suggested by folk medicine in India, where its topical application destroys bacteria which may have contaminated the skin.

However, the flesh of aloe vera has its own fresh, slightly "vegetative" scent, for which it may indeed be useful for cleansing an area through this smell alone- burnt aloe vera, however, smells disgusting. Unfortunately, drying aloe and using it for decoration would be near to impossible, given the fleshy leaves contain a great deal of water, and shrivel into twisted husks when dried.

Fruits of Eden, Herbalism and the Occult

African folk medicine often relies upon dances, ceremonies, and invocations, paired with its herbalism- and those practicing the more authentic version of hoodoo may encounter healing rituals which make use of aloe vera for its protective capabilities.

It should be noted that while consuming small amounts of aloe is normally not considered dangerous, and that there are actual recipes calling for its use, it is a mild laxative, which of course can cause its own negative physical effects.

ANISE
(pimpinella anisum)

Anise is a culinary (and potently medicinal) herb which has use dating back many centuries.

There is a tendency in ancient herbal lore to associate plants which have effects upon the reproductive system with protective powers- anise is an excellent example, as the fragrant herb has been used in some cultures to prevent menstrual cramps (although its use is largely discouraged in modern times, because it may cause toxic reactions.) It is used to flavor a certain socially imbibed liquor known as *Raki* in Turkey.

Anise, in protective charms, is normally added to a satchel bag, and kept on the wearer- as with many such herbs, where the fragrance itself seems to be the primary source of protection. The fragrance of the anise seed is used in an attempt to prevent hexes, and to break curses.

The anise may also be kept in a satchel bag under one's pillow- which may have its origin in its use (detailed in Greece) as a sleep aid in addition to its effects upon menstrual cycles.

A different species, *Illicium verum* or "Star Anise" is also used within occultism- particularly within voodoo workings where it is used to bring good luck and prevent hexes, functioning in a similar manner to *anisum*. It's possible that one was used first and that their similarity led to the other being used for such similar purposes. In some antiquated sources, species are listed by what we consider modern names, while being different species altogether.

Anise has also been added to ritualistic baths to purify the body- and some new age groups use it for aromatherapy- it is an easy to grow herb, which is grown in many gardens, but the drying process involves more than simply leaving the harvested parts in the sun, and the entire stem must be hung upside down in order to prevent a rapid decaying process from damaging the harvested material.

The extracted oil may be useful as an insecticide- repelling most parasitic life forms through a topical application.

BAY
(laurus nobilis)

The bay laurel is perhaps best known as a symbol of conquest and victory- awarded during Greek games to victors who had brought honor and glory to their people.

Fruits of Eden, Herbalism and the Occult

The symbolism of the bay laurel goes beyond merely a randomly chosen plant symbolizing victory (and thus the divine protection of the one bearing it.) Laurel is considered a protective herb in and of itself- there have been some claims that laurel was consumed by the prophets of Greece (particularly the oracle at Delphi) to encourage a sort of predictive trance, but it's not clear laurel itself contains anything that would cause such behavior- so any experience derived from it seems to be more occult than medicinal.

The connections Laurel had with various pagan sporting events (including the Pythian games) in the ancient world is intertwined also with its ritualistic use to increase strength (thus protecting an individual's health- as the two were seen as themselves paired.) The laurel is likely to have been wild harvested rather than deliberately cultivated for most of its uses, although the tree is certainly farmed.

In pagan mythology, it is considered to be the herbal counterpart of Apollo, the tale being that laurel first came to exist when a certain nymph was fleeing his advances, changing into a tree in order to confuse him- thus the bay laurel is also called Daphne.

The laurel is often used in aromatherapy- and it does have medicinal effects when applied topically as a poultice as well, whereby it is used to get rid of itching and skin irritation. The macerated leaves possess what may be mild antimicrobial properties.

Within the occult, it is most often used as a pure symbol rather than burned or used for its scent- simply possessing the plant is supposed to protect an individual- it may also conceivably be fashioned into a wand, or the wood used for other purposes, although it is not clear that such is traditional.

Decorations made from laurels, or headbands worn thereof, can still be seen in some neopagan ritualism, and for good reason given its fairly significant medicinal and pagan applications-not the least of which is the occult protection it imparts to the bearer (or wearer.)

BLACKBERRY
(rubus fruticosus)

The common blackberry is most often eaten as a fruit and not recognized as being spiritually useful in any manner- but it has been used before (in several ways) in occult practices. Wild-growing across large parts of the North American continent, is is abundant in marginal woodlands and sometimes infests areas- which is great for obtaining fruit but terrible to have to walk through due to its thorns (which are easily defeated with leather gloves.) The plant attracts bears, so we may consider it predictably identified with the latter in totemic manner.

Fruits of Eden, Herbalism and the Occult

Blackberry forms a large number of fairly pliable, long vine stems- as such once the thorns are rubbed off, or clipped, the yearling stems can be used as a sort of makeshift twine- something I myself have used in my occult practice, creating makeshift totems of wood and either blackberry stems or grape vines (depending on availability.) This process is alluded to in the not-quite-authentic *Blair Witch Project* numerous times- but the movie did get it right with regards to the basic construction of totems or standing charms to mark off an area as spiritually significant (solitary occultists or groups thereof may choose to deliberately include such unnerving imagery near their outdoor area of practice, specifically to ward off children or other unwanted visitors who may unwittingly observe things they are not meant to see.)

In English tradition, an archway made using live blackberry plants may be used to cure ailments- normally this living hedge is walked under, in hopes that the sickness will subside- there are also numerous tales related to individuals avoiding eating them after Halloween, the time of year when Lucifer supposedly "claimed" them and began to destroy them, having landed in a patch of such plants during his fall to Earth. This Satan-defeating plantwork is alluded to as well with Devil's Shoestring and other species in other traditions.

Tea made from blackberry leaves (which have a very mild berry-ish flavor) is favored by some as an aphrodisiac, or to increase general fertility or sexual function. The plant is also considered protective- and its addition around the fringes of ones' property is said to prevent harm (indeed, trespassers would likely not attempt to push their way through a dense growth of thorny plants to invade a home.)

Blackberry is useful in the creation of ink- along with black walnut and coprinus mushrooms, and may be leeched with lye for this purpose, creating a deeply blue, almost black, and high quality ink that is somewhat superior in quality to black walnut (which has a lighter, more brownish hue) and almost as good as, and far easier to create than, that from coprinus mushrooms. Blackberries are more often harvested from the wild than cultivated directly in some areas where it is native and tends to inhabit the fringes of tailored properties on the margins of forested land, without any actual attempt at cultivating.

BLUE COHOSH
(caulophyllum thalictroides)

Blue Cohosh is a fairly well regarded medicinal and occult herb- however it must be noted that pregnant women and children should not even handle the plant due to its toxicity.

Originally used by Native American groups, it serves a dual

purpose- one being medicinal, and one being occult (and the two, in some ways, overlap.)

Medicinally, the plant is used to encourage miscarriage of children- sometimes when mixed with pennyroyal tea in European circles, the two combining to create a fairly strong abortifacient effect (but which in the western world has been rendered unnecessary by the availability of surgical abortion which is admittedly safer.) In backwards areas of the world this method is still in use.

The natives who first cultivated the plant regarded it as protective (possessed of a protective spirit, possibly because of its use as medicine.) It is often grown purely for its spiritual potency, which it is said to impart in the area surrounding it. It is thus one of the more important species for a shady occult garden.

Sometimes, the stalks it creates (which are endowed with rather attractive blue berries) are dried and hung upside down to protect a room- sometimes used particularly to protect children, although care must obviously be taken that the child not have access to the plant, lest they eat it and become ill or pass away. It is also brewed and used as a sort of protective wash, although because of its toxicity this practice is in question as to usefulness. Here we see a strange situation; the stalks are hung to protect children, but the material itself when brewed is used to destroy a fetus.

Because it despises direct sunlight (and being dry it dislikes even more) it must be propagated within a shady area, preferably grown in clumps in a lightly forested environment- although artificial shade such as the north side of a home will protect the plant and usually result in a more moist soil which It will thrive in- I have found it a useful rule of thumb that if ferns favor an area, blue cohosh will most likely thrive there as well.

Because of the necessity of the roots not becoming dry it should not be placed within a garden in a raised bed- although it may be bordered with rocks or other materials to prevent it from needing to compete with other life forms.

CALAMUS
(acorus calamus)

As one of the most medically important plants listed in this work, calamus (sweet flag) has been used on three continents for its beneficial purpose, and has a fairly long history of religiously based, mystic usage.

Often used in Asian medicine and ritual, the plant was ingested for its sedative effects, and was actually used as a companion to shamanistic rituals involving mind altering drugs, to soften the effects and prevent intense or worrying hallucinations- the plant seems to have been used by Native American tribes for a similar purpose, applied topically to prevent fear in the face of battle.

    The number of possible medicinal applications of the plant are large in number- from suppressing cancer to antimicrobial action, for which this highly active plant is sometimes grown and harvested decoratively (including among native groups) to ward off sickness and evil- it is told that the plant was dried, stored, and steamed in a home to defeat illnesses, which was done in a ritualistic nature but also had the combined effect of releasing bacteria-destroying chemicals into the air, purifying the home using it. Like white sage, due to these medicinal properties, it is altogether possible that success was often had at such workings.

    Like irises, calamus prefers a very wet location to grow, and when planted with blue cohosh, irises, and cat tails, creates a spiritually significant wet-area garden which functions best for those with a swampy area on their property (including near drainage ditches.)

    In its penultimate show of occult potency, calamus is listed in *The Book of Abramellin* as one of the ingredients for the purifying oil listed, and can be used in ritual bathing before rituals are performed, or after they are performed, or alongside its ingestion to aid in bodily cleansing.

    The oil (in a manner not unlike dragon's blood or frankincense) is sometimes used for anointing an individual to protect or bless them- and the plant's fragrance is powerful, and is said to have been used in the medieval era to stave off plague by placing it in the home or church.

CHRYSANTHEMUM
(chrysanthemum sp.)

Chrysanthemum is a commonly grown, showy flower with a light, pleasant scent, and a history of use in Chinese folk medicine- particularly in conjunction with other herbs (especially onion and licorice) in order to stimulate energy in the body.

This practice of "warming" one or more centers of the Tan-t'ien (Dantian) but particularly the lowest of the three- below the navel- involves various combinations of herbal remedies, meditation, massage, and martial arts (or similar exercises such as Tai Chi.) The flower has a long and varied history of use- representing both good luck and death, depending upon the specific subspecies, and/or the culture in which it is found. In the Far East, it is normally reserved for funerary use. However, in the Americas, chrysanthemum is mostly considered a positive force, sometimes dried and hung in the home for good luck, and at other times the petals are strewn about to promote good health. Here we have two separate occult cultures, as they were, treating the same plant differently in their rituals both cultural and spiritual.

It is possible to brew certain species into a sort of tea or to use it for culinary purposes- such teas and foods are considered stimulating, warming, and generally beneficial for keeping sickness away.

The flower may have been adopted as a symbol of luck and prosperity in the west when it was found that brews containing fairly small amounts of the plant acted as a decent (and mostly nontoxic) insecticide to protect crops. The flowers contain pyrethrenes, which can be used in the occult garden as well, as a natural repellent and pest killer, without the dangerous side effects of chemical compounds derived from artificial sources.

Chrysanthemum also filters the air of pollutants, creating a cleaner space (similar to the boston fern,) and thus may be of use for those who favor a sterile zone for their rituals- although these effects will of course be blunted in an outdoor setting. It is a natural filter.

This flower is additionally useful in those practicing or studying Japanese mysticism or religion- for it is represented commonly in Japanese folk art, and used for numerous festivals and religious practices in that culture.

CITRON
(citrus medica)

The citron plant has been in use in the Mediterranean region for many centuries, mentioned by Pliny and, later, by islamic sources.

Reportedly used as an antidote to poisoning when steeped in wine, the shrub like tree produces a profuse number of citrus fruits. It is not able to be cultivated outdoors in any but the warmest climates. When used to prevent death or illness from poisoning, it acts as a purgative, the bitterness of the citron mixed with the sour nature of wine used, causes almost immediate vomiting (and is thus probably effective as an antidote for slower working, directly ingested poisons when administered with haste.)

The peels of citron fruits are added commonly to potpourri mixes- and it has specific mystic connections to Jewish festivals, which call for its ingestion along with various other foodstuffs considered healthy and cleansing in nature. It is additionally alluded to for mystic purposes at Egypt's *Karnak Temple*- a location of mystic importance there.

The scent of the plant is potent and said to be useful for cleansing the body and purifying the home when it is released- like calamus the peels may contain substances which exhibit antimicrobial action, so even when divorced of occult context, it is still useful for helping prevent illness.

Various pagan deities have been depicted (it is claimed) holding citron, or associated with its use- from both Vedic and European cultures- including Kubera (ironically connected both to evil and to wealth, depending on time period and philosophical school.) Some of these are speculative depictions and it is not absolutely certain that this species is being represented.

One variety used commonly in Chinese, Buddhist mysticism is referred to as "Buddha's Hand" and creates a fruit which has a plurality of extensions resembling fingers- although the plant also, with its numerous projections, seems to imitate a lotus flower as well, an additional connection to the eastern paths, for which it is regarded as a mystically important plant (although it seems to be used less as medicine or food than as an offering to Buddha, in this context.)

The plant may have been used as an ornamental, to attract positive energy and wealth to the home, and to repulse harm, in parts of then-Persian land, if Pliny's summations are correct.

CLOVER
(trifolium sp.)

Clover is instantly recognizable by it's large, triplicate (or sometimes four leaved) appearance, and its small round-ish blossoms which are swarmed with bees in summertime. Wild growing, it can be planted almost anywhere except for arid soil and do well, and even charges the soil with nitrogen, for which it can be used as an aid in restoring dirt which has been leeched by farming.

The most widely known use of clover in a mystic setting is for four leaf clovers, mutated leaves which are used as good luck charms, and may be allowed to grow on ones' property, or may be dried, added to jewelry, or simply kept in ones' wallet or pocket. It is also considered protective of a bearer in some folk tales.

Sometimes, mutated clover will grow in some areas but not others (for unknown reasons.) These lucky patches are generally considered best to leave in place and not disturb- some new age groups consider them a meeting ground for good spirits. Occasionally, 5 or even 6 leaved mutants appear as well (and in some folk tales, these are actually unlucky,) and the clover-resembling "sweet and sour" plants which infest gardens in the North Americas sometimes exhibit similar mutations.

An extreme example of the use of four leaf clovers would be to collect and dry a significant number of them, and then adding them to a satchel or used in some other fashion, perhaps powdered and added to a candle, or in some other way- however, the difficulty of finding them is substantial, for only one exists for every 10,000 or so normal clover leaves. There is a fairly small patch on my own property which contains an abnormally high number of mutants- probably closer to one in 100 leaves, and thus this small area I consider of possible occult importance.

Druids (at least in ancient times, possibly modern druids as well) had a tendency to attempt to use them to evade evil spirits- although the particular type of plant used in such an example is the shamrock, which is not the same thing as the clover more commonly found in the Americas or in other parts of Europe apart from the British Isles.

Clover is also thought to coincide with good harvests- and its use in dried form as a sort of magickal powder attests to such use- this may be due to its ability to fix nitrogen in its root system, thus increasing both the growth rate and yield of grain crops.

Those who wish to cultivate clover, as long as they do not live in a very hot or dry area, will find little in their way of doing so- the seeds are inexpensive, and the plants will grow voraciously, surviving repeated cuttings even on fairly infertile soil.

CORIANDER
(coriandrum sativum)

Coriander is a wonderfully fragrant, medicinal, and culinary herb, with both the seeds and stems/leaves commonly used in cooking. An easily cultivated species, it will grow rampantly in most soils and regardless of sunlight levels, as long as its delicate frame isn't crowded out completely by other species competing with it.

Coriander roots have an intense fragrance and may be extracted using alcohol to create anointing oils which are protective in nature- they may also be dried and used as decoration, while the seeds are almost equally scented and often used in potpourri, satchels, as food, or crushed and used as a culinary flavoring agent. The fairly hard-to-destroy seeds have been found in archaeological digs dating to ancient times all around the old world. They can literally persist under dry conditions for thousands of years, and remain viable.

    Commonly consumed as part of folk medicine from the east, it is said to cure sickness, prevent sickness from occurring (and may in some instances be consumed in quite large amounts) and purge the body of toxins. Like many ancient herbs and spices, it has been suggested by modern holistic medicine as one of a small number of plants which carries an abnormally large number of benefits, being reportedly both antimicrobial and anti diabetic. The plant also grows well when paired with anise (due to differences in nutrients required for strong growth) and so is easily added to the occult garden alongside it.

    In China, coriander is sometimes consumed in large quantities by pregnant women, in an effort to increase the intellectual capacity of the child- it is also indicated that the seeds may contain stimulant compounds (similar in strength to yerba mate or coffee) and so may become mildly addictive if eaten in larger quantities.

    In some British folk tales, it is powdered and kept in a bottle with other herbal substances (namely turmeric and ginger) in order to bring luck to the home. No further processing appears to be necessary in such tales.

CORN
(zea mays ssp.)

Corn is a widely grown staple food- in the modern age much of its spiritual significance has been forgotten as mechanized farming and genetically modified grain crops have replaced more traditional farming methods- but maize species have been used in ritualism for centuries (even spawning various deities associated strictly with the existence and growth of corn plants.) Easy to grow, corn of any kind is best grown alongside beans, which will replace nitrogen lost as the corn will tend to devastate soil after only a few years without either heavy fertilizer use, *terra preta* use (see the charcoal section of this same work for an explanation thereof,) or companion planting. Any of these methods can be used in conjunction for even greater ease of growth.

In traditional Mesoamerican culture, corn was often offered to various deities to ensure a good harvest, and subsequently to thank them if the harvest was indeed good- those interested in Mesoamerican mysticism will find numerous allusions to corn in ritualism and religion. In new age black religion, namely at Kwanzaa, *Muhindi* is a stand in for the celebration of children; making corn, there, a fertility symbol. Its phallic nature additionally belies its male character.

Dried corn kernels can be kept in a satchel and represent prosperity and protection from need and want- an extension of harvest ritualism. Importantly, the presence of corn in ritualism has stuck around even as the theistic meaning has been largely abandoned- decorations in autumn of dried corn stalks, cobs hung off doors, and so forth (along with pumpkins and gourds) are all part and parcel of the original, important rituals surrounding harvest. Whether we regard *Samhain* or *All Hallows Eve* or any similar folk tradition, corn and other harvest staples are invariably present.

Corn has a number of utilitarian uses as well which can be important for the occultist- the stalks can be cut into lengths and used as makeshift wands or staffs (depending on the type of corn these can be somewhat flimsy, or quite durable) while the cobs of corn can be used to create charcoal (in a manner similar to pine cones used for the same purpose) where wood is lacking for charcoal production. I have tested this method with my own corn cobs- it works quite well, better than pine cones and of extremely good quality, easily powdered for use as a soil additive.

The cobs can also be fairly easily made into pipes for smoking tobacco or other substances- and were used by natives during their own mind-bending rituals in the ancient past. The imagery of the corn cob pipe has its own Edwardian era importance whether occultism is regarded or not.

Fruits of Eden, Herbalism and the Occult

It is theoretically possible, also, to use corn stalks to create makeshift, temporary, and amusingly biodegradable altars or other structures, and the corn produced is of course fully edible- and generally of far better taste than corn purchased in stores. *Bantam* and *Silver Queen* varieties are generally best, and heirloom in origin.

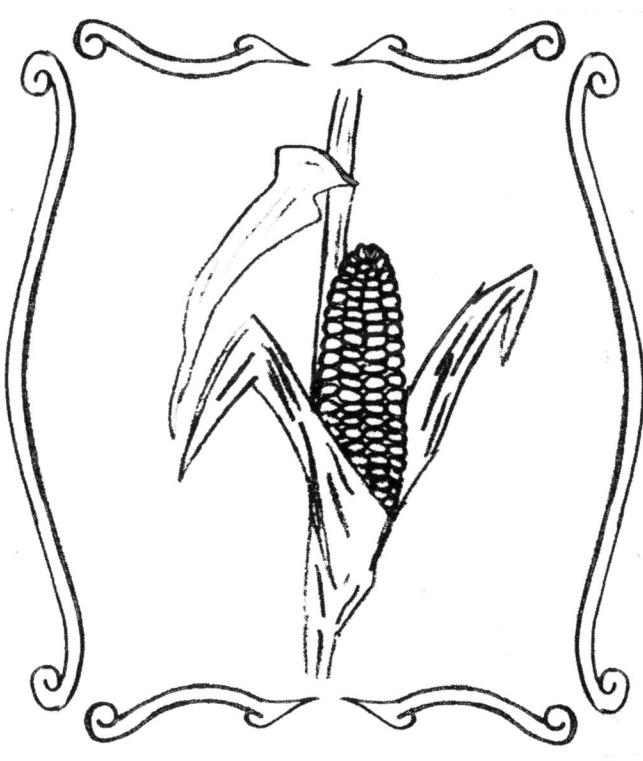

CUCUMBER
(cucumis sativus)

The common cucumber is not widely recognized as being a particularly important plant within the occult. Easy to grow (sometimes reaching gigantic sizes with little effort) it is usually known more for its role in "becoming pickles." Obviously, this section is not about occult pickling processes. However, the cucumber has several uses within a spiritual context- something largely overlooked by the occultists of the world.

First and foremost, cucumbers are known in Japan for their use in defeating certain water dwelling spirits (called Kappas) through simply writing one's name on the cucumber and depositing it in water which is host to the spirit involved. While most people in the modern age construe the kappa as a nonexistent physical being which ancient Japanese individuals considered to be an extant creature, it is just as easily construed as a sort of ethereal demonic presence found in stagnant areas of water (and is no less genuinely occult than stories of succubi or incubi inhabiting similar locations.) The Filipino spirit (sometimes regarded more as a vampire, lich, or demon) called the *Aswang* is most commonly defeated using garlic, but somewhere along the way, Japanese culture appears to have overlapped this foreign tradition and cucumbers are now also infrequently mentioned as an item of value in the same process. For those who wish to learn more about this intensely culturally important spirit, the *Aswang,* a very good documentary called simply "The Aswang Phenomenon" exists.

Cucumbers were worn by women who desired to become pregnant in the middle ages as well, likely because of their resemblance to a human phallus. Midwives seem to have had a similar tradition around the same time. Phallic symbolism and thus phallic-looking species of plant are very often identified with reproduction, children, child rearing, child protection, and similar phenomena.

Similar to aloe vera, cucumber has a soothing, anti-inflammatory (and possibly mildly antimicrobial) action when applied topically (and is often used in lotions for this reason.) Such use in folk medicine is common.

Possessing quite large flowers, this attractive plant may be grown purely for culinary purposes by most individuals, but its connection to preventing demonic attack, and promoting pregnancy,

Fruits of Eden, Herbalism and the Occult

places it squarely amongst the protective plants of the world. I have never found cucumbers particularly tasty on their own but some people will eat them by the dozen.

It should also be noted that certain cucumbers, which possess thicker outer layers of "skin" can be used much the same way as birch bark or toadstools in writing symbols upon them related to rituals- it could be adorned with such symbolism and then purposefully consumed by ritual flame, although it's unlikely most occultists have done so.

DANDELION
(taraxacum officianale)

Dandelions are edible, medicinal, mystically important in folk rituals (particularly from Appalachia) and easily grown- a sort of weed in most areas, and almost impossible to kill, with a deep taproot suitable for drought and a tendency to thinly colonize areas ranging from fields, to gardens, to alpine forests.

The plant is entirely edible (although not choice) with the root used in various teas, the flowers used to flavor certain Appalachian wines, and the leaves used in salads- folk tales from my own region consider the dandelion greens particularly beneficial at relieving vitamin deficiencies, with the root made into tea a fine addition to the diet for the benefit of sound sleep. Its sap is used at times for wart treatment (to varying degrees of success.)

The most common link between dandelions and love is simply the childlike ritual (which today is largely overlooked as authentically mystical) to blow off the seeding heads (which float through the air) after having said the name of a desired lover- and if the heads are all gone, you will be able to persuade them into a relationship. (This is somewhat similar to the practice of plucking flower petals to determine if another individual loves you.) However, the dandelion is more often seen as protective- its presence desirable both as a food source and medicine.

It has a more authentic link to the mystic though, with the roots thought to increase virility in men when tea is made from them- dandelions contain chemicals which control blood sugar (an imbalance of which can cause erectile dysfunction) so this claim is likely completely valid. It is highly protective of the liver and of the sexual system.

The flowering parts of the plant, similar to indian paintbrush, can be used to obtain dye through leeching processes- this dye is a very bright yellow. It should be noted, however, that many individuals (myself included) are extremely allergic to dandelion pollen and have a significant negative reaction to smelling or ingesting it. As such, I have never made use of them in my own rituals- what good is a protective plant that causes your face to swell and your sinuses to drip with a ferocity greater than if you snorted black pepper like it was cocaine? I have however sampled the greens in salad and they're extremely good.

In one folk practice, a large number of dandelion taproots are gathered together and boiling water poured on top of them- the fumes which are then released are thought to combat negative energy, as well as invite friendly spirits into the home.

DEVIL'S SHOESTRING
(viburnum sp.)

Viburnum (devil's shoestring) is related to honeysuckle- a vining, shrubby plant, commonly found in the wild but popular in gardens also- particularly the gardens of those practicing the occult, usually hoodoo or similar paths. While the berries of some viburnum plants are edible, most are toxic and should not be eaten.

The long, wiry roots of the plant are commonly used in folk medicine- extractions and infusions made thereof can help with menstrual cycles, and the roots are often used whole and dried, placed underneath a door mat in a literal attempt to "trip" Satan should his form attempt to enter a home. In some instances, the root is chipped into pieces, dried, and used as a magical substance in and of itself, and generally kept in the physical possession of an individual who wishes to protect themselves from demonic forces. In the African American mystic path, devil's shoestring is supposed to protect against goofer dust; a form of curse powder.

In an attempt to garner luck or wealth, or to prevent harm to the self, some individuals mix devil's shoestring with whiskey and either anoint themselves with it, or drink the concoction (not recommended due to possible chemical interactions) which is supposed to be very good for this purpose.

Some individuals choose to carry a single piece of viburnum root in their pocket to protect their money or to get mystic help for their career (in searching for a job, being promoted, or in similar ways) while others tie the roots around their ankle in a bid to prevent their enemies from ever being able to harm them. It is difficult to determine which specific rituals involving this practice are authentic, and which are trumped up by charlatans producing cheap pamphlets marketed under names like "The Amazing Godly Vine" or "Get Rich Fast with This Plant!"

Viburnum plants are fairly easily grown. Due to the generally uncultivated manner in which they grow, it isn't uncommon to find various subspecies in the wild (especially marginal forested areas) but cultivating the plant is as simple as putting root stock into the ground and watering it in- the plants do have a tendency to infest the land and spread rapidly, so pruning and weeding out unwanted growth is constantly needed.

DRAGON'S BLOOD
(daemomorops draco)

Dragon's blood is not itself a plant, but rather a resin derived from several species, but most commonly *daemomorops draco*, a type of palm found in Asia. Due to its need for a rather warm climate, growing such plants in Northern climes requires an indoor space- normally a greenhouse or sufficiently sunny room with south-facing windows.

The plant itself has a host of mystically useful qualities- firstly and most importantly, as a source for resinous dragon's blood (which coats the ripe seeds) which has a range of uses- as incense of course, but also in folk medicine as a balm for wounds.

Some groups consider dragon's blood of high importance in strengthening other spells (whatever those spells may happen to be) along with increasing the likelihood of a good outcome. At its core, the resin is considered to be virtually always a positive substance.

The seeds of this particular plant are also useful- beads formed out of the pea sized seeds are used in Buddhist prayer and meditation, in a manner not unlike that of a Catholic rosary. This is its most traditional use outside of incense scenting.

The resin produced on the outside of the ripe seeds is actually edible (although it contains little nutrient value) and has been used for medicinal purposes not just as a balm, but in ingested form, with the belief that this is a good general remedy for intestinal problems- however, ancient sources which cite the resin as useful for medicine, sometimes fail to differentiate between resin taken from different species, and in some cases, sources may be referring to cinnabar, a toxic arsenic containing mineral, or to other substances altogether.

In some circles, it is thought that both the resin itself (even when still clinging to the ripe seed) and the incense, increase fertility and sexual potency, and may be used in such a manner as well, in addition to strengthening other spells, or for protective purposes. The incense is said to be both purifying and protective, with the affected area shielded from astral, demonic, or physical harm for a period of time after burning it. Due to the huge quantity of dragon's blood available in the world, it is thus thankfully inexpensive and, in warm climates, grown easily.

In one final use, the resin can be dried, powdered, and formed into a sort of ink which contains a deeply red luster, making it useful for artistic work or sigils drawn for occult purposes.

EVENING PRIMROSE
(oenothera sp.)

Evening primrose is one of a small number of plants (along with moonflower) that flowers primarily at night- a native of Mexico and parts of Central America, now cultivated as an annual with ease in temperate climates, where it grows in most conditions as long as it isn't continuously wet.

Evening primrose, due to its nighttime flowering habit, is associated with the moon, lunar rituals, with feminine energy, and a style of maternal protectiveness. The flowers themselves are, either in living, potted form, or as cuttings, used for decorations on altars or in other areas to infuse them with positive (and feminine) energy.

Since its roots are edible and said to be pleasant to the palate, evening primrose is sometimes used as a sort of vegetable, but it contains chemicals which should be avoided by epileptics and those who are pregnant, for it contains anticoagulants and other compounds which could prove problematic for such individuals.

Importantly, the plant is often used in herbal bathing, where it is either boiled and the steeped fluid added to a bath, or where the flowers, dried or fresh, are added to a bath, which is said to protect and also increase sexual desirability towards the opposite sex.

Like parsley, it is said to help soften and open the cervix when administered vaginally, and has thus been used as an abortifacient aid, to cause miscarriage, although it is less often used for this purpose than parsley, which is more widespread in growth and easier to cultivate in an agricultural setting.

The flowers of the plant are also supposedly edible although of poor flavor, and the petals thereof are more often used as a decorative effect, and bring nightly energy and a positive aura where they are distributed or used in such a manner. Used in folk medicine to treat acne, eczema, and other skin disorders when steeped and used as a topical wash, the flowers are also used in the same manner in order to soften and moisten the skin, preventing repeated outbreaks.

FENNEL
(foeniculum vulgare)

Fennel has a triple use in folk medicine and within the occult- three different cultures which each lend it a usage, from Greece, the East (mainly India) and American folk magick (which may have its roots originally in Britain.)

Fennel, which is a hard-to-kill sunshine loving herb (with one species, the florence fennel, used as a vegetable, all other species valued for the seeds or extracted essential oils thereof) was used in Greece (and thus, likely, other nearby areas) in ancient times to craft wands or staffs- the variety used was much larger than the type naturalized in the Americas, however, being of a giant cultivar. These wands were used in lieu of the latter-day witch hazel during this time period, and were important in the fabled rites of Dionysus, in which feasting and wine was indulged upon as part of orgiastic fertility rituals (and fennel, being medicinal, certainly was thought helpful for fertility.)

    In India, fennel is more often used as herbal medicine for Ayurveda, replacing some pharmaceuticals in rural areas- it is both a diuretic and cough suppressant, and reportedly also useful for repelling parasitic insects. It is thought to have a sight-enhancing quality, which figures heavily in certain American (and likely originally British) folk tales.

    The American variant of its use seems to originate in Roman Britain, where fennel was made into tonics and applied in drops to the eyes (and it may in fact prevent or treat glaucoma.) The American variant involves collecting dew from the leaves of a fennel plant (sometimes only at night, sometimes only at a crossroads, and sometimes both) and using this to anoint the eyes in an effort to preserve eyesight. It's not clear if this has a basis in actual medicine, and with some variants the dew is collected from the fennel flowers or seeds rather than the leaves of the plant.

    The American variant of this use may have crossed with the use of dew from spiders' webs which are used for very similar reasons. A variety of folk charms involving fennel seed as an additive for satchels or other herbal applications or objects also exist.

    The plant is also used in a culinary manner, most commonly with the crushed seeds added to food to flavor it (and its flavor is similar to that of anise, which is also a mystically useful herb.)

GARLIC
(allium sativum)

Of all protective plants, the use of garlic is possibly the most widespread, persistent, and remarkable of all- it has featured heavily in modern herbal medicine and in herbal medicine from the past, along with both ancient and modern occultism.

Garlic is most commonly known as a deterrent to vampires- those occultists that believe in spiritual (or physical) vampirism may make use of garlic during their craft, in the same way that Eastern Europeans made use of it as a sort of blessed charm, whose potent scent was rumored to stave off nocturnal assault by both vampires and other beings or spirits.

Being exceptionally easy to cultivate (in any soil it produces a plurality of bulbs that, when separated, can form a large patch within a few short years if not over-harvested) garlic is a prime choice for a cheap inclusion should a magician desire to make use of it. Those venerating Hecate as a deity should remember that the Romans offered garlic on stone piles to her.

Garlic is thought to be stimulating and warming towards the body, and may be useful in lust related magick as well as that which is protective- roasted garlic seems to be used more often for such purposes. It is most often allowed to form "bulbs" and is subsequently strung up on doors or windows in a home to protect it against spiritual attack- it also has an incredibly long history of use as an herbal medicine (not just in a culinary manner, but ingested also as a supplement or infusion.)

Within folk medicine- which seems to now be present on all continents- it is used to destroy a fever, prevent colds, stop headaches, to prevent boils, acne, and other discolorations of the skin (through topically applying it) and as a repellent for most parasitic insects (as well as to destroy tapeworms and other internal parasites.) It does indeed work for this, and is capable of causing such intestinal worms to exit the body, tormented by the volatile oils produced by the garlic on its own and during digestion.

While modern medicine recognizes only a small number of its medicinal uses, garlic features so heavily in both folk medicine and folk magick that it might be said to be the most renowned of all occult plants. The essence of garlic is far too pungent to be added to incense or potpourri (without burning the eyes at least) but it is still used mainly for ingestion or for its scent.

Garlic also seems to have been used by some plague doctors of the middle ages, apparently thinking the scent was powerful enough to destroy the evil miasmas of death that permeated their area- this might have actually been somewhat effective if the individual were to ingest large quantities before they were infected, as it may in fact repel fleas- large amounts of garlic may also have repelled rats, perhaps further inducing the prevention of sickness.

HOREHOUND
(marrubium vulgare)

One of a host of medicinal plants now recognized by modern science, horehound has been used since ancient times as a folk medicine for lung complaints and is considered edible.

The plant itself is stalky, has a minty fragrance, and tends to spread in a manner similar to spearmint, often infesting gardens where it is not controlled in growth- it attracts a host of beneficial insects as well, making it valuable when placed in an occult garden. Pollinators adore horehound.

Horehound lozenges are often sold to treat cold symptoms- mainly a sore or dry throat, and also a cough (and it works well for this purpose.) However, it has two more mystical applications, beyond merely folk medicine.

The first involves a tea made from the leaves or flowering parts of horehound- this brew is said to increase mental clarity significantly, and to bring on a state similar to catnip tea, in which the body is very relaxed, but the mind is very alert- useful as a meditation aid, or to bolster the overall mental state before rituals are performed. I have not tried horehound tea for this purpose (although I have used catnip in this manner) but people who have used it swear to its efficacy.

The tea which is made from this plant is also said to be useful for encouraging deep, prophetic, or lucid dreams, and to aid in astral travel. The state which it encourages helps the mind to delve into the subconscious.

Horehound may also be used as a protective charm in the following manners- either that the essence of the plant be extracted and added to incense (where it works almost as a reverse dragon's blood, dulling magickal potency directed at an individual or home) or used as a fragrant body wash which is said to be physically exhilarating as well.

Some new age groups link Horehound with Horus, and the use of such a plant therefore, to them, is linked to the veneration of this particular Egyptian deity. This is not specifically authentic, but is practiced as though it was.

Horehound contains antimicrobial compounds, and as such incense burned containing its essence may serve some purpose at eliminating disease from the home, sterilizing the area in a manner similar to the burning of Juniper or steaming of Calamus.

HYSSOP
(hysoppus officianalis)

Hyssop is a shrubby herb, ironically mentioned in the bible, where a wash of hyssop is said to cleanse an individual until they are "whiter than snow." It is grown easily in most climates, is fragrant, and has a very long, and quite varied history of use in both folk medicine and mysticism.

Fruits of Eden, Herbalism and the Occult

The biblical mention of hyssop is mystic in nature itself- for body washes made from a steeped hyssop admixture have been used for centuries in an attempt to purge sickness and ward off evil- or to prevent sickness, or to clean the body physically of pollutants.

Hyssop, however, also has another connection to the mystic realm, containing thujone (the same absinthe-related compound found in certain wormwood species) and can be considered a possibly mind altering substance- however, other chemicals present in the plant render it useless for psychedelic experiences (and are particularly bad for epileptic individuals.)

The fragrant flowering stems of the plant may be gathered, hung upside down and dried, and used as an exfoliant before a ritual steam bath, brushed on the skin to open the pores and cleanse the epidermis. The dried herbal material can be chopped roughly and added to a satchel or used in potpourri to prevent harm to an individual.

Hyssop has also been used to purify places of worship, or places of ritual practice- the usual method involving either incense (or directly burning the herbal material itself in raw form) or else a wash made using the hyssop which would be used to anoint important locations.

It is thought to reverse or destroy curses and hexes by some new age groups, which either partake of aforementioned ritual bathing, or else burn hyssop to shield themselves from attack. There are many mentions in more modern circles about a ritual in which the individual (who believes themselves cursed, possessed, or generally in bad luck) bathes in water which has been infused with hyssop (sometimes with other herbs present as well) and proceeds to take a portion of the bath water to a crossroads, where they either throw it over their shoulder or deposit it in a bucket, after which their curse or bad luck is thought to be broken. Whether such a ritual is entirely modern or was taken from a folk magick system of older origin isn't clear.

Hyssop has been mentioned as a good addition to blessed or holy water, which is then used itself to sanctify a place of worship or ritualism, to bless another person or thing, or to exorcise evil spirits.

JUNIPER
(juniperus sp.)

Juniper is an excellent plant when used in the healing arts of the occult- some claim that the higher survivorship rate of patients in Swiss hospitals during various conflicts were due to the burning of Juniper wood in the hearths- which released antibacterial vapors which prevented wounds from festering and helped patients with infections of the lungs.

Fruits of Eden, Herbalism and the Occult

Common Juniper is fairly widespread in cooler climates in the Northern Hemisphere and does particularly well in higher elevations, easily growing to a decent size and yielding not only a high quality wood (which can be used to create altars or wands or similar implements) but numerous small, blue "berries" which are used in both flavoring foods and for various herbal medical applications.

Juniper is useful in medical contexts due to its powerful antimicrobial action and its (supposed) usefulness in contraception, for which it was utilized by certain Native American tribes- being applied, normally, to the vagina before intercourse (although it is not certain it works.) The spice taken from crushed juniper cones is also used to flavor gin.

It is also useful in bonsai, which can be peripherally related to any eastern spiritual path requiring patience, focus, feng shui, or meditation.

Juniper "berries" (usually in whole form) are sometimes kept in one's pocket to protect against harm (particularly, diseases) and may be used solely as an aromatic substance to discourage the entrance of sickness into a home. Sometimes, the juniper is mixed with other healing, protective herbs or substances such as anise, forming a powerfully fragrant mix.

Various balms used for skin complaints and to dress wounds have also been traditionally made to include crushed juniper, or sometimes resin taken from the actual plant.

Juniper plants can be easily grown in cooler climates in either hemisphere despite being native only to the Northern hemisphere- if the temperature becomes too warm, the plants will normally die, and they cannot tolerate extreme drought- however they are extraordinarily slow growing and, thus, extremely long lived, and will persist longer than most humans if not destroyed by predation or disease.

LAVENDER
(lavandula sp.)

Lavender is notable in both historic and modern use, exceeding most other herbs (unless they are being ingested for folk remedies) in their scope of availability- easily grown almost anywhere where the soil is not extremely wet, it is exceptionally fast growing, fragrant, and useful- it makes a beautiful and helpful addition to any occult garden.

The flowers of lavender are commonly kept in raw form in potpourri, or dried and hung in their rather long stalks, bundled together to enrich a home with their scent- or they may be used in dried form kept around the home, on or under the bed, or on the magician's person to protect them from harm- it is very commonly added to incense, both for its own scent and to sweeten and compliment incense blends.

    Used in both ancient Egypt and Rome as both temple incense and for herbal medicine, lavender has a large number of uses- for healing abrasions and skin rashes by reducing itching, and as a repellent of certain insects such as mosquitoes- it is also a sedative and relaxing agent, and tea made from the flower heads is fully edible- it has also been (occasionally) mentioned as a flavoring agent in certain culinary traditions.

    Lavender incense is particularly potent and used in aromatherapy and in rituals which are meant to calm the occultist, or others, or to uplift the mood- it is a cleansing agent as well, thought to purify the body, and as such the flowers may be added to a bath, or the essence thereof added to it.

    Lavender also has fertility connotations (as do many fragrant flowers, especially those linked to the creation of high quality honey, as lavender definitely is) for it is used commonly in both floral arrangements and otherwise, in weddings in parts of the western world- however it does not seem that lavender has been used in folk magic to increase fertility.

    For occultists to whom vivid or lucid dreams (or long periods of restfulness) are necessary, lavender acts as a catalyst for such things and is potent at the same level as passionflower for this purpose- it alleviates insomnia as well (which, in my personal experience, has come in handy, for my own insomnia is exacerbated by ritualism at times.) It additionally helps to decrease pain due to muscle aches- and may thus help those who meditate for long periods but have any form of extant clinical disorder that causes such pain.

    Lavender tea is not only tasty, but is good for the common cold, helping to get rid of congestion- for those practicing with sonic magick or who intend to read long or multiple invocations, this aid is invaluable.

LEMON BALM
(melissa officianalis)

Lemon balm is exclusively used within the occult as a protective herb- it has a significant history of being used in folk remedies both extracted and in its raw form- it isn't that uncommon for people to rub the leaves on their skin (some people have an allergic reaction to it) in order to prevent insects from getting on them- it does seem to work against mosquitoes and black flies (in fact, citronella, which the plant produces, is extracted and added to mosquito-repelling torches.)

When used as a protective herb within magical systems, it is generally grown around the home, in hopes that its (pleasing) scent will purify the air- it is antibiotic (although only slightly) and so it is possible that the vaporized oils from the leaves of the plant do at least slightly block the propagation of microbes.

The herb is also used in aromatherapy and homeopathic medicine as a mild mood enhancer, which is meant to relax the individual. Sometimes the herb is dried and kept in a satchel, or strewn about the home, for similar effects to growing it in fringe areas near the house itself- it may also be used purely for the enjoyment of its fragrance without any spiritual or medical necessity thereof (a sort of feng shui solely for the relaxation of the occupant.)

When added to herbal tea, in some folk remedies particularly from North America, the plant is thought to be a sedative on the same order of potency as chamomile- a mild action somewhat weaker than one would achieve using Valerian.

Lemon balm is especially fragrant in the autumn, when its flowers bloom and (literally) drip with sap which contains a great deal of fragrance- the plants will dry out after frost comes, and these dried stalks retain most of their fragrance as well. Since the dried, dead parts remain fragrant, a large bed grown near the home will continue to provide fragrance well after a frost.

I have lemon balm growing in my own garden- it is tolerant of almost any conditions but prefers at least partial sun. If it gets too wet, its root system will be destroyed by bacteria rather quickly.

MARIGOLD
(tagetes sp.)

A widely cultivated, easily grown flower, marigold comes in many varieties and is an entirely beneficial plant when grown. It repels deer and certain insect pests from the garden when grown on the edge of the same, and provides a great deal of decorative (and extremely ritualistically significant) color.

In Mexican culture, marigold is intricately associated with the dead- and so while the plant is helpful for necromancers, it is more often used as an offering *to* the deceased, to pacify and bless their spirit, to prevent them from wandering aimlessly and thus accidentally (or purposefully) bringing harm to the physical world, all while keeping their needs cared for as well. A medicinal tea made from certain variants of the marigold plant in Mexico (*lucida* subspecies) may have a mildly psychedelic or hypnotic effect and is supposed to relax the mind and allow the drinker to see visions of the future. Ornate flower-based decorations for the Mexican Day of the Dead often include marigold wherever yellow or orange is needed.

As an anti-inflammatory and mildly antimicrobial plant, infusions made from marigold are often used in folk magick in Mexico and elsewhere to treat wounds, which helps ease pain and swelling and to prevent infection- tea made from certain species is thought to strengthen the composition. It is also reported to be a strong aphrodisiac, thus useful for sexual ritualism (if indeed it acts in this manner, which is disputed.)

The same Mexican variant (*lucida*) that is used as a psychoactive by certain native groups is more potently antimicrobial than other species- and as such is likely more useful than the more commonly grown varieties of the Northern regions of the Americas at wound dressing. Elsewhere, marigold is mostly considered decorative alone, unless it's being used as a sort of fragrant border to, again, repel deer.

Marigold flowers can also be processed into an extremely bright yellow dye- and while the art of making and using dye is mostly lost today in favor of chemical washes in industrial centers, those who wish to take up this skill will find marigold a fairly simple source of this color, whether for occult purposes or not.

It is fairly difficult to kill marigold plants unless they are repeatedly flooded by heavy rain or attacked by insects- as such it is a potentially important addition to the occult garden.

MUGWORT
(artemisia vulgaris)

Mugwort (also called common wormwood) is a highly medicinal plant used in folk medicine- having a large variety of herbal uses. It has several spiritual uses to its name as well.

Easily cultivated in most climates, mugwort will grow virulently and spread rapidly, colonizing fringe areas and becoming a noxious weed which will choke out other plants if it is not controlled and kept to one area. The occasional wormwood stalk appears in my own garden, and if left alone they will quite literally begin to resemble

Fruits of Eden, Herbalism and the Occult

a small, licorice-smelling pine tree.

Mugwort contains the same psychoactive chemical (thujone) as absinthe wormwood, albeit in smaller quantities- however care must be taken if making use of the plant for its divinatory or protective powers, because of its thujone content.

Normally, the plant is made into a dried smudge (similar to those made using white sage) and is lit and blown or waved out, allowing the smoke (which is purifying) to scent the home, moving from room to room to protect each in turn.

It has also been mixed with tobacco (notably, sacred or aztec tobacco) and smoked, to obtain prophetic or divinatory powers- this is discouraged due to the possibility of dangerous psychotic reactions.

In Roman times, mugwort was added to sandals or boots in order to prevent cramping and aching feet- this use is quite legitimate, considering that mugwort is an effective (if mild) anesthetic, and helps to numb pain- for which it is applied topically in macerated or infused form to other body parts as well in herbal medicine. Some are allergic to mugwort, and as such a medical professional should be consulted before such herbal remedies are applied.

The stems of mugwort plants can also be used to create easy-to-make wands; for this purpose it is second to none in ease, for simply allowing cutting the stem and allowing it to dry finishes the process. Interestingly, the other primary source of wands apart from carving them from wood itself, is the very next plant (mullein) in this alphabetically ordered section.

Pregnant women should not ingest, inhale, or even touch mugwort- it contains chemicals which can stimulate contraction of the uterus, possibly leading to miscarriage (although oddly, mugwort is linked to the goddess Artemis, and to child rearing.)

MULLEIN
(verbascum thapsus)

The common mullein plant grows wild (without any propagation whatsoever) throughout most of the Northern United States and into Canada, although native to Europe and North Africa- a pestilent biennial weed, it will invade garden areas and is particularly fond of disturbed roadside areas where other plants will not grow. It will take over infrequently mowed lawns, and produces tens of thousands of seeds from even one neglected plant.

The flowers of mullein have been dried and smoked by Native

Fruits of Eden, Herbalism and the Occult

Americans for centuries as a treatment for asthma (in my own anecdotal experience, it works, although not very effectively.) More reasonably, herbal tea can be made from its flowers and is drunk for a similar effect (or to relieve coughing, for which it is second to none.) The plant is technically edible in small amounts, but possesses a terrible flavor.

Used since the times of ancient Greece to ward off evil of all sorts, an individual may choose to bathe in water that has had mullein steeped in it, or may rub mullein leaves on their body- it can also be carried in a satchel but it tends to fall apart into dust when dried for any period of time.

Some European folk traditions include mullein as an effective way to prevent an individual from falling into harm by placing mullein leaves in their shoes.

Interestingly, the mullein plant has a very utilitarian use within the occult as well- the dried stalk can be separated into lengths and then used as candle wicks (for which it is reportedly good.) The leaves contain "fuzzy" hairs which are irritating to the skin of some individuals, so if they are to be used for tea or any other purpose, it ought to be filtered.

In African traditions, a substance called "goofer dust" is sometimes used to curse enemies- some recipes call for a mix of grave dirt and powdered, dried mullein, and may also include salt, red pepper, sulfur, or dried blood.

Instead of using mullein stalks as candle wicks, the entire stalk can also be used as a gigantic incense stick in itself (the plant sometimes achieves nearly six feet in height) simply by lighting the top on fire, then blowing it out and allowing it to very, very slowly smolder- the smoke arising from this is thought to be highly protective.

I have crafted wands from mullein before; it is far, far easier than using wood or any other material. I will explain more about this process later in this work. In brief; the stalk is cut down when the flowers begin to brown and turn to seed pods, the seeding part removed from the stalk, and it is cut to length and allowed to dry in the sun. After drying to a light brown it is rubbed with sandpaper to remove the hairs (otherwise it becomes a dust and hair magnet) until smooth. Over a month or so it will continue to dry, eventually becoming slightly stronger than balsam wood and about as light. Dozens or hundreds of wands can be made in this manner quite effortlessly in a single day.

Fruits of Eden, Herbalism and the Occult

PARSLEY
(petroselinum crispum)

Parsley has a strange history, being one of the herbs most reviled (along with mandrake) by medieval and renaissance era society, while at the same time having various medicinal uses- the superstition surrounding parsley almost makes it worthy of mentioning as useful for black magick, but it seems links between parsley and the darker side of the occult are largely baseless and were formulated by the church, attempting to discourage its use.

One medieval tale tells of how parsley's roots grow literally "into hell" and that using the plant causes either death or the destruction of the soul (which must have shocked groups that had been eating it as a garnish for some time.) Greeks predating christian times also avoided parsley, seeing it as a death-related plant and involved with the story of *Archemoros*, the forerunner of death.

Medically, it has two major uses- the first as an antioxidant-packed culinary ingredient which today is used heavily in European dishes, with the second being that ingesting it (or using a bundle of parsley applied vaginally) can encourage miscarriage- which may be why it was reviled, for in the medieval era such medical practices were certainly seen as Satanic. (As such, pregnant women should avoid ingesting large amounts of parsley. As a garnish it appears to be generally, medically regarded as safe.)

Parsley is sometimes braided and dried into various charms which are worn to preserve strength and to prevent illness- less often it is dried and strewn about a room as a protective charm, although if one subscribes to the Greek system, this may have the opposite effect and bring an aura of death upon the home.

In some folk tales, parsley is used to prevent an individual from getting drunk- although this seems limited in range, with the herb more often being used for abortifacient effects, or as a simple stand-alone charm.

In a strange twist, parsley is associated with fertility (creating fertility) and with child bearing, protecting children, and so forth, even as its use in more ancient times was largely to discourage fertility or to destroy the embryo. It isn't entirely clear where this switch from child-destroying to child-protecting occurred. This is similar to the story of blue cohosh mentioned previously.

Uprooting the plant directly is said to be bad luck (possibly because of medieval European allusions to its roots stretching to the infernal realm) in some folk magick systems. Most often, among such groups, the parsley is rather slashed off near the base and allowed to wither and rot. Identifying parsley being uprooted with bad luck or death may have been the result of a confusion with mandrake at some point.

Parsley is very easily grown and will function as a biennial in southern climates, tolerant of almost any condition except quite prolonged drought.

PENNYROYAL
(mentha pulegium)

Pennyroyal is the third of the abortifacient herbs, used alone as a tea, or brewed with blue cohosh, sometimes with parsley or secondarily while using parsley vaginally to soften the cervix. (Such herbal methods are mostly outdated.)

Mostly, when it is not being used for herbal medicine (as either an abortifacient or to settle the stomach) it is dried and kept in bundles to protect luck and to prevent illness- sometimes it is powdered and mixed with other herbal substances (notably nettles) and sprinkled on the body (although the addition of stinging nettles to the mix may cause irritation of the skin.)

Easily grown as long as it isn't crowded out or subjected to excessive heat, pennyroyal was often grown in the gardens of midwives before surgical abortion was common and while herbal medicine was used by most populations- oddly, like parsley, it is also seen as protective of a pregnant woman, for while when ingested it can cause abortion, when used as a mystical charm it is said to protect the unborn child and the mother both against harm.

Pennyroyal is also spoken about in folklore (particularly of European origin) as a doubly-useful herb for those intending to travel long distances- some is placed in the shoes to prevent the feet from tiring, while some is sprinkled on the individual, or else offered to the saints or various deities to ensure safe arrival.

In a manner similar to white sage, pennyroyal is sometimes dried, bundled into a roughly cigar-shaped "smudge" and allowed to smolder in a manner similar to that of incense- it is used for roughly the same purpose (although it has been eclipsed by white sage in popularity among most occult groups possibly due to the more pleasant scent of sage) to purify a given area of demonic intrusion, or to lift the general "aura" or mood of the home, or of a room, or of an outdoor area.

It should be duly noted that extracted pennyroyal oil is extremely toxic, and should never be ingested or used without medical supervision- and that even long term use of weaker infusions of the herb can cause liver damage.

Like its ability to stimulate abortion, pennyroyal is sometimes used as a contraceptive (I do not recommend this in any manner) by continuously stimulating the menstrual cycle, although because of the danger of toxicity, this is a fairly uncommon practice except in third world situations.

PURSLANE
(portulaca olaracea)

While most plants which are used or useful for occult, ritualistic, and folk-medicine practices are cultivated and agriculturally grown, purslane is itself an invasive weed (although not a particularly harmful one) and is edible, containing immense quantities of vitamins and minerals- and is even companion-grown with certain weak-rooted vegetables to allow them to break through hard soils.

With a flavor similar to spinach when cooked, and an unidentifiable, slightly "salty-spinach" taste when raw, purslane is not a particularly showy plant, with tiny flowers and succulent leaves-however this largely unnoticed weed is medically active and spiritually potent, even mentioned by Pliny for such purposes (and to wear as a protective amulet said to ward off evil intent) in his *Natural History*. I would rate its flavor as generally favorable, and it's as easy to grow as simply leaving it alone to grow on its own between rows of vegetables or flowers wherever the soil is not too dry for it.

It is easily cultivated from seed, but it tends to eventually show up in small numbers in all gardens, and by allowing it to flower and go to seed, it will eventually spread over soil, preferring raised beds where moisture is drained easily. It is best when gathered in the afternoon, after a day of sunlight has reduced the acidity of its fleshy leaves.

Purslane has no real fragrance (although when crushed it smells vaguely similar to aloe vera) and thus is useless for incense, but crushing the leaves yields a slightly gelatinous substance which, when added to a bath, invigorates the body. It contains a small amount of dopamine and noradrenaline, and as such, consumption of small amounts of purslane are a mild mood enhancer as well. It is best eaten cooked, because raw purslane contains chemicals which may exacerbate or create kidney stones (it also enhances the flavor substantially) but it can be eaten raw in small amounts as part of a healthy salad. As a garnish, it is not only flavorful, but even causes the food to look more attractive.

Amulets can be made using strung-together portions of weaved and subsequently dried purslane stems (either with or without the leaves attached) which, similar to the mention of such charms by Pliny, protects the wearer from evil in Aegean traditions.

The plant can also be gathered and burned over charcoals (preferably natural or homemade lump charcoal rather than briquettes) with the smoke thought to purge evil spirits from the home. This can be done in conjunction with lavender or white sage for an increased wholesome effect.

ROSEMARY
(rosemarinus officianalis)

An entirely beneficial herb, rosemary is used frequently as a spice in food, and forms a somewhat shrubby bush or small tree over time in warm climates, grown as a smaller herbaceous annual in colder ones. It will easily grow in loose soils, especially with full sun, and resists some level of drought.

I have grown a great deal of rosemary for its scent- growing it near the home washes it in positive energy, and fragrance, which is mentally clarifying. It is linked with two religious traditions- the first being that it was first formed when Aphrodite (the Greek love goddess) was born, and the second being linked to it's name, loosely "Rose of Mary" after the mother of Jesus.

    Rosemary is used in teas and foods for detoxification- perhaps because of its insane level of antioxidant compounds which can destroy free radicals in the blood. It has been used (either alone or infused into alcohol) for centuries as a tonic, body wash, and medicinal balm. In the account of *Don Quixote*, rosemary, along with wine, oil, and salt, create a sort of balm with miraculous powers (and while the story itself is fictional, such balms were common during the time.)

    Rosemary is not solely used for balms and fragrance, but is also used to obtain love and procure a mate- especially in medieval customs where it was used in various ways for divination and to charm others into marriage- these customs culminated in its common appearance in modern weddings.

    It has also been used to prevent demons or other evil entities from harming children, simply by hanging rosemary above cradles- and in a similar manner it can be used to prevent bad dreams, although in such folklore the bad dreams are often sent by demons as well. It was additionally used in Egyptian embalming formulas- with the ability to help prevent decay over time by curing the flesh- it is unclear whether this facet of the plant has ever been used in necromancy.

    It may be added to a hot bath in cut form in order to ritualistically cleanse the body of impurity (and the mind or soul along with it.) This process may also involve the ingestion of tea containing rosemary- and it does have a mentally stimulating medicinal action.

Fruits of Eden, Herbalism and the Occult

SAFFRON
(crocus sativus)

Saffron is perhaps the most valuable spice in the world- commanding an insane price for even a small amount of stamen material (the part of the plant usually made use of) for culinary, or medicinal purposes.

Largely grown in the middle east, saffron's medicinal traits were well regarded enough that Buddhist monks most often wear robes which are the color of these stamens (often, the robes being literally soaked in a saffron solution to dye them) perhaps due to some sort of mystic use in the past of the herb- bright red, and intense golden yellow, being the two colors associated with the saffron crocus.

The plant is able to be cultivated in warmer climates around the world, but the yield of usable material is so scant that hundreds would need to be planted for even a small harvest- a few acres of saffron crocus would be worth many tens of thousands of dollars due to the nature of the plant- the stamens have to be snipped and dried entirely by hand, because the process is too delicate for machines.

Saffron was used in healing (and spiritually protective) baths in Roman times- with wealthy individuals regularly bathing in hot water steeped with a small amount of saffron, thought to prevent illness and bring wealth (a self fulfilling prophecy at times- for only the wealthiest could afford such a luxury.) Importantly, during the age of the black death, saffron was thought to both prevent infection with the miasmas, as well as to treat those who were afflicted (which, like with other herbal remedies prescribed at the time, likely worked fairly well given its very real medical potency.)

Used for everything from bleeding to infected wounds (or internal infections) saffron was extremely important in ancient times for medical use- one explanation for its existence coming from Greece, where a certain tale tells of a youth named (aptly) "Crocus" who is cursed by a wood nymph and turned into a flower.

Saffron is, today, often grown in small quantities for its use as an herbal medicine (or as an extremely profitable herbal crop) although its largely vegetative propagation and its need for well drained soil make it somewhat more difficult to grow than other crops (although bulbs can be obtained easily.) Because of the expense involved, I have not experimented with growing this particular type of crocus.

It has also been made into healing teas- or the stamens may be dried and added to other herbs to form a protective (and very expensive!) balm imbued with its own spiritual powers.

SASSAFRAS
(sassafras albidum)

Sassafras has a double use- one protective and one somewhat more malevolent, depending on the herbal school making use of it, and depending upon the individuals' intentions.

It is largely a wild, uncultivated plant, but it can be naturalized to a garden location as long as it is wooded or kept at least partially shady- and it will grow in most climates as long as it isn't bitterly cold- usually by vegetative propagation of the roots, which are also the part used within the occult rituals associated with the species.

The roots are sometimes made into charms- kept in a bag or else made into jewelry- sometimes to protect the wearer, or more often to increase luck and wealth within voodoo circles- but they are also used in rootwork in attempts to curse enemies, sometimes involving an image of the enemy, or else a prayer or invocation. An enemies' name may be carved into the somewhat woody root and the root consumed by fire as with any other material used in image magick.

Sassafras roots are sometimes dried, cut into small chips, and used by more mystically minded individuals to attract wealth and health to their home or place of business- although unscrupulous merchants have been known to chip apart any woody root at hand for such sales.

The leaves are also useful, more for culinary purposes however, for they are used to thicken and flavor certain southern foods such as gumbo. It is almost worth adding sassafras to the mind altering section of this work, for the roots contain safrole oil- which is used in the production of MDMA (ecstasy) but it is more often used as a root charm by people who aren't manufacturing large batches of drugs for sale. Officially, sassafras is in a legal gray area for cultivation due to the presence of safrole (although the drug enforcers decided this was on the basis of safrole being carcinogenic, rather than hallucinogenic.)

Sassafras plants are relatively uncommon in northern climates, being most common in the deep south where weather is more favorable, and as such some individuals may simply purchase the roots or dried materials rather than attempt to propagate it themselves (considering that a hard late frost will butcher them.)

Connected to fertility, the roots of sassafras were once used as a treatment (and sometimes cure) for sexual diseases in the 17th and 18th centuries, thought to be effective in dealing with gonorrhea (in addition to reducing fevers- for which safrole-leeched root material is still used in some herbal remedies.) It is fairly useless for the former, but for the latter may have some effect- when we speak of 17th century sexual disease treatment, we're speaking about an era in which tin syringes were inserted into the urethra and random compounds injected into the urinary tract- sometimes cinnabar in solution with other materials.

SUNFLOWER
(helianthus annuus)

Most often grown for its edible (and rather tasty) seeds or as an ornamental plant- sunflowers actually have a fairly long history of use in spirituality and ritual magick. Grown with exceptional ease in most decent soils, it is popular among gardeners for incredible size. (I have grown sunflowers that achieve eleven feet in height with no fertilizer at all.) It requires only that nearby weeds or grass be removed.

Native American groups fairly early on realized that sunflowers were useful in the veneration of solar (or astronomical) forces- while the mature heads do *not* as folk tales suggest, follow the sun through the sky, the buds and very young blossoms do- and thus it was quickly adopted as a solar symbol (also likely because it simply resembles the sun- corona and all.)

It is thought by some new age movements that merely growing sunflowers near the home will charge it with positive energy- it also has a number of medicinal uses within folk magick, the most lauded being its use in removing snake venom from a recent bite area (for which it was applied as a balm to draw out the toxins.) Often used as a replacement for peanut butter, sunflower butter is usually praised for its flavor, and has documented health benefits.

The heads are sometimes cut off before the flower begins to wilt, and hung in the home both for decoration and to drive away negativity- to protect the home from being destroyed, ransacked, or otherwise disturbed. The stalks of the plant can, like mullein, be used to make candle wicks as well, and even pressed into a form of rudimentary paper, which can be cut into lengths after fairly simplistic processing, and thus used for work involving sigils or invocations which the occultist may desire to write on something other than commercial paper.

As a replacement for other woody and "generally" straight stems or woods for wand making, sunflower could be quite useful for rituals related to solar deities, astronomical forces, and "white" magick. The process for the same is similar to that for mullein. Unfortunately, a powdery brown "pith" inside the sunflower stalk makes for a wand which will eventually be attacked by rot and end up hollow. My experiments with partly carbonizing the same to prevent rot have, to the present day, failed.

Generally, the seeds themselves are not used in mystic workings- however they can be used as a fertility symbol for ones' craft, and utilized in a manner similar to other herbs (and, because of their content of unsaturated oils, their use in food may stave off impotence.) Most often, the flower's head or the stalk is used in occult work.

THISTLE
(cynareae sp.)

The entire thistle tribe is bristling with medicinally potent and spiritually active members- however the the milk thistle, and the burdock plant, are most concerned with such use, with other varieties

Fruits of Eden, Herbalism and the Occult

largely linked to those central uses.

The milk thistle (s*ilybum marianum*) is very important in medicinal use- even in modern times, studies have shown its effectiveness when taken as an extract, in preventing and repairing damage to liver cells- it is able to treat hangovers, and the flowers are easily dried and kept around the home, working in much the same symbolic way as other thistle plants, to protect the home, and the individuals therein (although the flowers have no fragrance and so are not used in incense or similar fashions.)

Milk thistle extracts are also used often in conjunction with the spiritual use of amanita mushrooms for spiritual purposes- the thistle extract prevents mortality by protecting the liver, which can be damaged by use which is too frequent or when the dosage is too high.

The burdock plant (*arctium lappa*) is even more spiritually important- the roots thereof are quite large in the plant's second year (it is a biennial which flowers the second year of growth) and quite woody, allowing them to be carved into amulets or charms which are thought to be protective when worn.

The roots are also used in tea which is common in folk remedies from North America and Europe- it is thought to detoxify the blood (although excessive use causes hot flashes) while a wash made from the macerated roots, or from the leaves, can be used to clear the skin of rashes and other chronic problems. The roots are also a starchy vegetable with a flavor similar to potato, when scrubbed and boiled. This flavor is considered excellent.

Both milk thistle and burdock are extremely easily grown (burdock itself is a pestilent weed and spreads easily, so it must be weeded up before it is able to produce its seeds to prevent it from taking over a garden.) A sunny area is preferable, although they will grow almost anywhere as long as they are not subjected to arid conditions.

Care must be taken in not confusing rhubarb (which has poisonous leaves) with burdock- it is however fairly easy to tell them apart when they flower, as burdock produces a multitude of small, stereotypical thistle-like blossoms, while rhubarb produces a normally singular long stalk upon which a large, often malformed-looking flower is held.

VIOLET
(viola sp.)

There are many variants of violet, most of which grow wild and may be considered a weed (despite its attractive flowers.) It has been used in multiple folk traditions, is important medicinally, and will grow almost anywhere with ease.

Many species of violet are antimicrobial- as such it is often grown in windowboxes or around the home in an attempt to prevent sickness- a fringe of violets or windowboxes filled with violets is supposed to protect from home invasion. The flowers may be preserved by candying them, and then kept in the home as a mildly fragrant potpurri, or worn on the person in various forms for protection.

Violets are also used in tea although not commonly- such teas in folk tradition help to cure illness and strengthen the constitution- normally the flowering parts are dried and infused into hot water along with lavender for this purpose. Violets grown in the garden may help to protect against certain plant parasites which would otherwise attack other organisms.

The plant also has a significant connection to fertility and femininity (being associated with Venus) to the protection of children and of pregnant women, to the procurement of love or lust, and to the retention of sexual drive and vigor- teas and washes made using violets (and usually lavender) are said to help for all of these purposes, although pregnant women ought not consume violet tea or any other herbal remedy without consulting a medical professional.

Those who wish to attract butterflies and other beneficial pollinators to their garden to in turn service other plants ought to consider planting a fringe of violets around the garden (or, if they are growing wild to begin with, the area can be partly cleared and violets encouraged to spread in such areas.) The leaves are fully edible and can be used for salad.

The flowers of viola species are sometimes used purely for decorative enjoyment- the creation of a positive, decorative space for outdoor meditation, yoga, or other relaxing practices can incorporate violet flowers in large numbers, creating an extremely fragrant, self sustaining scent factory rendering incense unnecessary.

WHITE SAGE
(salvia apiana)

    White sage, native to the rather dry foothills of the Rockies, will be hard to cultivate in more rainy climates, but the supply of this plant is virtually limitless due to its tendency to spread voraciously. It is among the most important and widely used protective plants.

    The most common usage of white sage is in incense- it has an extremely powerful scent, which is thought to repel evil spirits, clean the skin, and improve the mood- like juniper and several other plants, antimicrobial compounds are released upon burning white sage, which quite literally cleans the area it is being used in of bacteria which may be harmful. The smoke smells vaguely like burned, low quality marijuana, in truth, and is quite thick when sage is burned or smoldered.

White sage is also fairly commonly found in smudge form- a bundle of dried plant material is gathered together into a tightly packed, roughly cigar shaped but larger bunch, and the tip lit and waved out, allowing it to slowly smolder and release fragrant smoke (this is the method employed by Native groups, who did not use charcoal based incense blends.) This smoke is quite thick, very cleansing, and thought to aid in the process of exorcism as well, being an order of magnitude more potent than a simple incense stick alone.

While white sage, which is difficult to propagate, is the best for creating smudges for exorcism or purification rituals, common culinary sage which is grown easily almost worldwide can be substituted, although its fragrance is not comparable. Those living in drier climates can easily propagate white sage from seed.

Tea made from white sage, as well as several other species, aids in relieving sore throats, both by soothing, decongesting, and destroying harmful bacteria which may be causing it.

This species is not thought to be psychoactive like *salvia divinorum* which is listed separately- and does not cause psychedelic reactions when burned and inhaled. It is also not considered edible, unlike common *salvia officianalis* which is so often used in the cooking of meats and certain pasta dishes in Mediterranean cuisine.

The plant is still to this day sacred to certain native tribes of the Southwest United States. People are highly discouraged from collecting large amounts in this region, both for fear of over-harvesting, and to prevent them from accidentally invading native land in their hunting for incense ingredients.

Fruits of Eden, Herbalism and the Occult

CHAPTER THREE
Plants grown or used for curses and necromancy

The ability to use herbalism is not limited to helping individuals, but may be used for quite nefarious ends- to destroy, curse, and of course in the process of necromancy.

ASH
(fraxinus sp.)

Although the wood of ash trees is not used strictly in curses, it seems to be fairly common for occultists to construct altars using its wood- and there are significant Norse connotations with the ash tree that go back to quite ancient times.

Firstly, that within Norse mythology, the world-tree Yggdrasil is an ash- a gigantic ash tree upon which existence hinges and is connected. I have also studied some of the Norse linguistics, and it seems some groups within Norse paganism believe the Norse race to have developed, in an archetypal manner, from ash trees, with other groups developing from other species.

Oddly, despite this wood often being used to construct altars upon which will be conducted what the lay-folks would call "black" magick, ash is also alluded to as highly protective (possibly figuring into some ritual systems, in which the occultist themselves must be protected by the very forces they invoke.)

This particular tree may have been particularly chosen for a great deal of occult work involving the crafting of wooden implements in part due to the ease of carving it, yielding a fairly rugged object which will stand up to wear as well as time.

Fruits of Eden, Herbalism and the Occult

Interestingly, I can remember back to the latter part of the Satanic Panic period in which some folks in the new age community were selling "witchwood" necklaces and charms, which were made from the wood of ash trees, and while the necessity of such amulets was negligible at best, the usefulness of ash as a magically protective plant is quite common to rituals and paths.

Within magick, however, in some cases and schools of occultism, there is a process of *inversion* used to either create or block negative energy- for example in New England, where horseshoes are considered good luck and often nailed above barns- such that an individual who wishes to curse their neighbor may invert the horseshoe, or else place an inverted horseshoe somewhere on their property, usually on a tree or buried near their front step.

Similarly, ash appears to serve the purpose of protection primarily not to protect others, but to protect the occultist while they practice what others would consider negative magick, cursing other individuals while preventing themselves from suffering ill effects.

In a tale similar to that of the crucifixion of Jesus, Odin was supposedly hung off Yggdrasil for nine days in agony, for the purpose of imparting the knowledge of language to the world.

Interestingly, mountain ash is said to be specifically important, and able to protect against lightning. In homes of Welsh origin, it is common to see mountain ash planted near the home; my own home, in the past, had two of these same trees next to the driveway, presumably for this superstitious reason.

FALSE DITTANY
(dictamnus alba)

This seldom known plant (as opposed to the medicinally important Dittany of Crete) serves various occult purposes- and has a mythological connection to the bible as well. I have some growing in my garden for various purposes.

Firstly, the chemical compounds present in the plant release a rather noxious gas that is literally able to be ignited once the plant is of significant size (or if the plants are present in large enough numbers.) The gas, once ignited, releases a fireball which may or may not destroy

Fruits of Eden, Herbalism and the Occult

parts of the plant itself.

This species has been suggested as the true root of the story of the burning bush found within Exodus- and it's actually possible given that the natural range of this plant extends well into the middle east. Oily compounds present in the leaves do not need to be ignited by a lighter but can roar into a fireball on a hot enough day as the result of a spark or perhaps a chip of reflective rock positioned in just the right manner, focusing sunlight into the foliage.

Perhaps because of its noxious nature, this plant can be used in curse work. In fact, most of the plants used in curses seem to have some underlying explanation (toxicity, or something else) for their usefulness, although to say this is the only reason for their negative effects would be outside of occultism.

Of special interest is that this particular plant, when powdered or made into an infusion, is useful in preventing wounds and sores from putrefying because of its severely antibacterial action- in the same sense, it can be useful for necromancy of the most literal sort, and may be used for a type of herbal mummification or to prevent a corpse from decaying while it is in use, without damaging the corpse itself. While it is the *mandrake* plant etymologically compared to the hand of glory present in the *Petit Albert* (one of several French grimoires) it is false dittany that would likely be of greater use in fixing the flesh used to craft the object. Generally, though, the hand is pickled.

Its presence across most of the old world (Europe, Africa, and Asia) means that it was used by, or could have been used by, many of the ancient cultures which would have found its chemical actions of particular interest.

In specific, its use within the field of curse work seems primarily limited to using its oils to supply light for a ritual space, or else (in the modern age) to burn an image of one's foe, a common practice used during invocation to use negative forces against them.

FUMITORY
(fumaria sp.)

The fumitory herb, also known as earth-smoke, is one of the more important plants for those who intend to mix their herbalism with the use of cursework or black magick in general- both protective and malicious, fumitory may be variously used as incense for altar or temple cleansing, consecration of ritual tools, or to destroy evil spirits, but it may also be used to curse, or in the process of necromancy. Easily grown but hard to acquire, fumaria seeds are typically absent in most seed catalogs and online stores. There are several subspecies.

Fruits of Eden, Herbalism and the Occult

Incense made using fumitory has been used in Catholic services in order to prepare and ritually clean churches- it has also been indicated in exorcism rituals, the basis for the same being its thick scent, which is thought to be torturous to demonic spirits.

Fumitory burned in incense, smudge, or simply dried form, upon an altar, produces a thick smoke which may be used in consecration rituals for wands, chalices, daggers, or other ritual implements- it may be used to cleanse robes or other clothing as well, removing energy from them either positive or negative, and re-balancing them for further use (for those who keep energies in mind within their rites.)

Steeping dried fumaria materials in a bath before rituals, and using the bath to purify the flesh and spirit, is thought to be a good practice as well. This prevents any prior action or intent from interfering in the present ritual. Interestingly, fumitory herb is also considered a good way to increase focus during rituals or rites, by temporarily alleviating earthly desires for material wealth or sex- as such it should not be used before or during any orgiastic rites, or rituals which revolve around sex or lust.

While fumitory may be mildly poisonous (and thus should not be ingested) it seems inert when burned as incense or in other forms, and a wash made from fumitory herbs can be used to clean the skin of blemishes, as has been done in folk rituals for centuries.

Fumaria species will grow rampantly and self-seed but because its herbal use is limited (and perhaps because its cultivation was dominated by the church using it for incense) it remains relatively uncommon, and I have found no reliable, constant source for fumaria seeds anywhere in the world- and other species which are referred to as fumitory (but which are different species altogether) are instead sold, which can confuse buyers.

HELLEBORE
(Helleborus sp.)

    Hellebore (even its name) evokes visions of black magic- and this is not a surprise, given both the appearance and toxicology of the plant. In modern times, we are reminded that it's quite possible that either black (and true) hellebore or some variant of white (or false) hellebore may have killed Alexander the Great.

    Growing in shrubby, overgrown woodlands and creeping along the ground with impressive but often dark blossoms, hellebore is quite poisonous, although its medicinal use has been documented for as long as it is mentioned in human record.

    I have not heard of hellebore being used in incense or in candle making, but it is sometimes used in summoning rituals, through burning it upon an altar- and the seeds are supposedly used in rituals as well (at least among Greeks in ancient times) but the ingestion of hellebore is unlikely to be part of any ritual, considering its potent nature. Propagating hellebore is presumably quite difficult given the difficulty in finding seeds for it other than a few variants- and planting it would require a sufficiently shady area (preferably away from wildlife or children which might attempt to consume it.)

    In latter times, hellebore as associated with the occult may be partially the fault of medieval citizens and rulers who came to associate anything toxic (and some plants which are not toxic but were thought to be) with witchcraft- for the hermits growing these things must have had nefarious motives. However, I do know that some black magicians stock hellebore specifically for summoning purposes- and it is available to purchase, although normally not in large quantities (possibly because the plant is so small in size.)

    Oddly, hellebore is also associated with what one might consider a white-magic event, for it is told that one little girl in Bethlehem at the birth of Jesus didn't have anything to give to him, and cried on the ground, and a white variety of hellebore sprouted from her tears (which of course is a story of dubious sourcing.) This folk tale perhaps predates its general use in what we might consider modern or post-Renaissance occultism.

HENBANE
(hysoscyamus niger)

Henbane has such a long history of use that it is hard to trace its exact origins.

What is known is that it was (or likely was) the active ingredient in "witch oils" used during the medieval times by the botanically inclined for ritual purposes- although the cultures of such time periods felt that these herbalists were actually dark occultists who killed off their grains (and amusingly, a different force- ergot, also occult in nature, was the real culprit.) Some have claimed the slightly less poisonous *Datura stramonium* as the source of witch ointments, but it seems more likely that henbane would be used since it is more concentrated.

Henbane can be feasibly added to incense or candles for its slightly lackluster scent. It isn't clear if being near the smoke of such candles or incense can harm the individual, but all parts of the plant contain an insanely powerful hallucinogenic compound called scopomaline that makes magic mushrooms look tame. As a pestilent plant, it will freely sow itself even in a dense lawn and persist for several years due to its seeds being capable of delaying germination for a generation or two. In this way, henbane can appear not to have sprouted, and the subsequent year several plants will grow, and the subsequent year, others will grow *even if the former generation was entirely destroyed.* It can take over fallow areas in just a short two or three seasons and must be controlled. Birds may eat the seeds and then excrete them, leaving patches of henbane in random locations.

It is said, by medieval sources, that the seeds, if smoked, can make a person go literally insane, although it is somewhat more likely that their "insanity" is a temporary state caused by the scopomaline- but anyone using henbane repeatedly in their rituals does run the risk of a genuine psychotic breakdown. The visions seen on henbane are not like those of typical psychedelics, but are far more involved and "seemingly real."

Even the presence of the plant is considered negative- and while it is a very attractive plant, some do not grow it, either because of the toxicity or for this reason.

Typically, for ritual use, if it isn't being added to a candle or to some form of incense, the plant is dried and placed in a sort of satchel (small bag) and left somewhere within proximity of an individual to be cursed- although in a confusing twist, some people actually carry it around themselves in order to discourage witchery.

Fruits of Eden, Herbalism and the Occult

    This process is common to both Africanized, hoodoo/voodoo rituals, as well as western occultism- for while the use of henbane seems most likely to have been European in origin, its use has since been absorbed into other groups and spread out to become a fairly common feature for occult paths in other parts of the world. Its ability to both curse and protect from a curse is interesting to say the least.

TOADSTOOLS
(Various tree dwelling fungi)

    Toadstools have an extremely long history of association with the occult.

Fruits of Eden, Herbalism and the Occult

Part of this is derived from Hollywood imagery; the image of a toad sitting upon a mushroom, once a prince but cursed by evil magick and forced to suffer until kissed by one of many princesses in the land. However, there is a genuine basis for the use of toadstools within occultism, for reasons somewhat similar to the use of birch bark by certain groups. It is perhaps worth noting that almost no species of tree-dwelling fungus is very poisonous- most varieties are simply inedible because they are primarily composed of a substance similar to the tree bark to which it clings. It would make you vomit, but not because of poison, merely because it is incapable of being digested.

Generally, within folk magick (and this is something that I know has been done around rural New England) the toadstool is inscribed with an enemies' name and then burned- it may also be marked with a foes' name, and subsequently buried with other herbs. The burning method is more common.

Folk magick from the area also includes the usual stereotypical "bury it at a crossroads with your enemies' name or something they own to prevent them from harming you" ritual. When I say "my region" here I must be clear that the lineage of folk magick I am accustomed to is that of New England/ Appalachia. The tiny sliver of valley and hill land running on either side of the Connecticut River has a subculture different from that of the rest of the states to which it is connected. This largely rural zone has similarities to the Appalachian lore which may be found elsewhere in the same mountain chain and its offshoots all the way down to the Ozarks, and is perhaps culturally more similar to parts of mountainous Virginia or Maryland than to enclaves of New England only a few tens of miles away from the Connecticut River itself.

This form of hex does not require a lengthy ritual, but the toadstool can also be used for more lengthy workings, even burning or carving on its soft underbelly a sigil and used for evocation work- this naturalistic crossover of a ritual which more often involves a papyrus or cloth is equally natural. Birch bark, previously mentioned, is also fine

Fruits of Eden, Herbalism and the Occult

for such workings, but it is the toadstool which carries the ever-present "dark" imagery.

Of course, it's possible that some of this ritualism evolved from assuming that the mushroom itself was poisonous- certainly such was the case in the involvement of *Amanitas* within occult imagery, but it does have a very real use in folk hexes. These presumably date to at least the early Victorian Era.

For obvious reasons, cultivating toadstools would be difficult and impractical for the occult gardener- but particularly in wet, swampy areas, they are quite common, ranging in size from the very small to the extremely large (several feet across.) Dead or dying trees are often slowly subsumed by toadstools as their bark begins to decay and fall off.

The environmentally minded occultist should make sure not to over-harvest in a particular area, for they tend to grow very slowly and in some areas can be considered rarities due to climate.

It is also important to note, that not every flat tree dwelling mushroom is a toadstool- typically, the ones used in ritualism are hard on top, white or yellowish underneath, and look almost bark-like on the top side, while the bottom is cool to the touch, firm, and white or yellow. They often grow in groups, but sometimes enormous singular specimens can be found on very large, dead trees.

WITCH HAZEL
(Hamamelis sp.)

Witch hazel is sometimes considered a protective plant, but as with the ash tree, the smaller witch hazel tree (which contains several species within its genus) has a dual use, being both protective as well as potentially malevolent in nature.

Like ash, it is most commonly used to create implements rather than being used in a ritual on its own as with some plants, and both older texts like the *Grand Grimoire* and modern groups (including some wiccans) regard it as particularly useful in the creation of wands.

Fruits of Eden, Herbalism and the Occult

The wand (which may or may not be used depending on the occult school) is, like any other occult implement, able to be used for evil intent- the primary use of this species being that the negative energy created is not accidentally funneled back to the spell caster, protecting them from harm even as they bring harm to others.

The wand, of witch hazel or any other type of material (wood, stone, crystal, metal) is essentially a directing rod- which may be short or long, decorative or plain, and which is used to direct energy in various ways.

The wood is also used for divining rods- sections of wood which may be used to find water (which is disputed in usefulness.) In my own anecdotal experience I have never encountered a dowser which possessed any specific, "real" capability whether they were using wooden rods for this purpose or copper implements, which have become more common over time.

Along with its medical use as an astringent, the wood may also be used for ceremonial fires (oddly echoing the use of ash wood) for pagan celebrations- certain astrologically important rites based on the coming and going of seasons, lunar cycles, and so forth.

In some occult groups witch hazel's dried leaves are burned on charcoal as a form of incense, and this is supposed to be highly protective in nature, along with encouraging the formation and distribution of energy. This ability could in theory be coupled with the simultaneous burning of "negative" herbs (or the presence of, say, grave dirt) to more easily allow curses to be made.

Because witch hazel grows wild in so many regions, cultivating it is usually not necessary, although live plants may be obtained. Many people will find it hard to identify the witch hazel tree; that is, until it bears its seeding bodies, which when perturbed can suddenly give off a small pop and fire their seeds out several yards.

Fruits of Eden, Herbalism and the Occult

WOLFSBANE
(Aconitum napellus)

In a manner similar to henbane, wolfsbane may have been used in certain witch oils (flying ointments) in the Medieval era and into the Renaissance.

Its use in curses is quite old- and its use as a toxic substance (literally to kill wolves, and often to kill people) is frequently documented. The plant contains an ungodly amount of atropine, and is able to kill within a very short span of time if ingested in large enough amounts.

Unfortunately, wolfsbane (perhaps because of its name) has been stolen largely by Hollywood as the standard "wizards use it" herb- and misconceptions of its nature persist and propagate among the population, from the silver screen to the pages of paperbacks which extol its supernatural character.

Even the long form of the Wiccan Rede mentions wolfsbane:

*"Widdershins go when the moon doth wane,
and the werewolf howls by the dread wolfsbane."*

Regardless of whether we identify Wicca primarily as a form of paganism now modernized, or a modern movement with vague references to authentic occultism, the mention is still there. The identification of wolfsbane with werewolves may be due to its subsequent identification with actual wolves in Europe poisoned by its compounds, or possibly because ingesting it may cause hysteria and animalistic delirium, or perhaps some combination of both, but the use of wolfsbane as a deadly toxin, and for dark rituals, is so well documented that even Hollywood hype and fantasy has not tarnished its use in actual occultism. It is an attractive plant, to boot, although one which will kill anything that gets into a patch of it.

Again, as with henbane, the plant may be added to candles or to incense, however, some tales suggest that even being near enough to smell the plant may cause heart palpitations, so its use in either is in question- and as with any substantially toxic herb care must be taken not to touch it without gloves.

Cultivating wolfsbane is actually fairly easy, although the seeds are not as easy to find as some plants, and must be cold stratified (a process involving refrigerating it for some days before planting them) in order to be viable.

YEW
(taxus sp.)

Yew trees (of various kinds) have a fairly long medical history. Some of the toxins responsible for fatalities from consuming the seeds of the plant are also responsible for treating cancer- for which Yew derived compounds are second to none; an example of holistic, originally occult medicine being proven absolutely correct. The compounds inhibit mitosis (the splitting of one cell into two cells)- and in cancer, the condition is the result of uncontrolled mitosis, in which cells split into oblivion, becoming useless and choking out healthy tissue over time, destroying tissue and organ alike.

Fruits of Eden, Herbalism and the Occult

Perhaps because the seeds prevent cell splitting and can put a person into a coma, it has been linked with the process of necromancy- it's entirely possible that such references are in relation to real events where a person slipped into a coma (and was thought dead) and subsequently "woke up from the grave." In this manner it is similar perhaps to certain hoodoo methodologies of the same type.

Yew wood is also, much like witch hazel, sometimes used to create wands- and yew has been used for many centuries as a sort of guide for the recently deceased, left at tombs in order to gain the dead entry to the next life.

Raising the dead is often a complicated process- it may take one of several forms:

A zombification, resulting in a person who is in a trance, still alive, but who acts like they are nearly dead, and who may show physical symptoms as though they were deceased. They may thus have a much decreased heart rate, weak pulse, shallow and slow breathing, and be largely unresponsive to speech, or even pain.

A metaphysical revivification, in which an individual is called forth from the grave through scrying or a similar method but not in a physical form- in essence, calling upon their spirit. They are thus what the mainstream individual would call a ghost, wight, or shade.

A physical revivification, in which an individual is quite literally brought back from the dead- in which yew is concerned, used as a sort of wand during these rituals.

Some occultists scoff at the very idea of necromancy, seeing a possible value in communicating with spirits, without actually believing in the notion that a corpse can be revived- but such events are at least claimed to be true in certain Renaissance era texts, again with the connection to science that in some cases it may have been the result of medical, rather than magical, action. In the case of these bygone eras it hardly matters; in those days, medicine as we practice it now (and which occultists then practiced it as- literally, "real" medicine as opposed to then-accepted quack doctoring) would be considered, and the occult medicine *was indeed* considered, "witchery."

CHAPTER FOUR
Mind altering plants and fungi

The use of mind altering substances is intertwined heavily with occultism- and while I cannot legally recommend that the occultist ingest any mind altering substance, I can discuss their traditional and/or modern use, and in some cases my own experience during a period of time in which I experimented with certain substances within a spiritual context.

BLUE LOTUS
(nymphaea caerulea)

The blue lotus is one of the more important spiritual plants- not only has it been used for centuries in the creation of perfumes and scents for ritual purposes, it is also a sedative (and, in my experience, a hypnotic.)

It is alluded to in Homer's Odyssey, as a plant which, when eaten, produces extended sleep or periods of lethargy- which makes sense, since it sedates the user. With the Iliad proven to be based at least partially on reality (Troy existed, and the siege of Troy actually happened) it isn't unthinkable that the core of this epic was, as well, based on actual history- we might envision an Aegean island to which the species was native at the time, and the sailors thereupon gorging on the same, putting themselves into a slightly hypnotic trance.

I have found this particular plant extremely useful in invoking the power of Egyptian deities- minds-eye visions are not all that uncommon with its use, and while it is typically brewed into a tea or else steeped in wine for a period of some days to extract its alkaloids (the tea and wine methods both taste awful) it can also be smoked, although the smoke is variously described as "harsh" and "of a poor flavor."

Interestingly, the plant is increasingly recognized by mainstream science as having medically significant qualities, including not just sedative properties, but antispasmodic ones.

Although it would be difficult to propagate this water-dwelling plant without a pond and a proper subtropical climate, the materials used for ritual purposes are neither hard to find nor very expensive, although it seems the stamens of the plant (in a manner not unlike the collection of saffron stamens) are far more hard to find than simply the mixed flowering parts, dried for ease of use. When found at all they command a higher price per ounce.

On one particular occasion, while making use of blue lotus, I had a vision of some sort of Egyptian god, with blue skin and surrounded by a golden light- whether this was subconsciously derived, or the result of the alkaloids present in the lotus itself, is not entirely clear. Nonetheless, others I have spoken with who have used the plant have reported similar strange thoughts while using it.

The lotus is excellent in creating a tranquil but focused state of mind and, because it does not seem to interfere with rational thought, some people may find it useful during meditation (and indeed its use in aromatherapy seems to indicate this fact.) It is possible to release these materials as a vapor by merely steaming them away as well.

I would warn the reader not to attempt to extract the plant into wine in order to ingest it- the resultant extracted mix is extremely bitter (even after straining off the soaked plant materials) and is nearly unpalatable in quantities necessary for it to have any effect- not to mention the alcohol may interfere with a pure experience as well, rending it more an intoxicant than a sedative-hypnotic.

Some report similar bad tastes using the tea method- in which the dried flowering parts of the lotus are boiled and then allowed to steep for a period of roughly 15 minutes- although I have not personally attempted and verified that this method works or the flavor thereof. This species is generally legal in most parts of the world. US law does not include it on any drug schedule.

BUNDLEFLOWER
(desmanthus illinoensis)

This particular plant may be classed along with mimosa and psychotria as containing DMT- a potent chemical which is often used in sacred rituals involving a substance called "ayahuasca" which is both medically and psychedelically significant to native tribes in South

Fruits of Eden, Herbalism and the Occult

America.

The bundleflower, and other DMT containing plants, is normally either brewed with other plants which complement it, or else larger quantities are extracted (which involves a fairly complicated chemical process) yielding a potent hallucinogenic crystalline substance which is more mind warping than even large doses of LSD.

The shaman of these tribes consider the ayahuasca brew (for they do not extract the chemical DMT itself to use in a pure form) a gateway to the spirit world- and anyone who has used ayahuasca and had it work, understands this claim to be quite realistic (or seemingly so.) For example, multiple users, across various cultures, report seeing strange strobe-like objects while under the spell of this witches' brew, which speak into their mind and encourage them to literally create things with their speech or song- a strange event referred to as "machine elves." The user's surroundings glow, morph, shift in form, grow and shrink at a whim, or become a void altogether. Strange voices are heard, and the entire experience is long lasting, unlike that of DMT alone, when smoked in pure form- the latter experience lasts at most for a half an hour, often less.

To the psychonaut these spiritual experiences may be considered more mundane- but within the occult it is fairly clear that this substance, much like salvia (which will also be listed in this chapter) opens up the mind to astral travel, or at least communication with astral entities. These forces should not merely be seen as delusions, but rather as spirits, wights, shades, ghosts, or something of that nature. The new agers may consider them ambassadors from some other dimension.

Bundleflower is not only a common plant, but it is almost a pestilent weed and grows in prairies and brush-choked areas all across the central United States- it is also available in fairly large quantities from herbal goods vendors on the internet, and is presumably able to be propagated in most temperate climates- although only the root bark contains enough of the substances in question to be of much use (much like mimosa species in Australia.)

    Although *psychotria viridis* is usually mixed with *banisteriopsis caapi* in authentic ayahuasca rituals, most individuals use either bundleflower or mimosa root bark as a replacement for psychotria given the greater ease of propagation, and the higher yield of available DMT in the plant itself- caapi vines may also be replaced by syrian rue- which contains the same complementary chemicals- namely MAOIs.

    It should be noted, however, that any occultist wishing to partake in an ayahuasca ritual ought to study the process in great detail before attempting it, as it is time consuming and could be dangerous if fairly strict rules are not followed- or the batch may be useless and cause no effects. Additionally, ayahuasca is illegal in most of the world- ayahuasca tourism thus exists, allowing westerners to use them in their literal native context. Most ingredients in these brews, on their own, are legal, however; I know of no law against owning or propagating Syrian Rue or Psychotria, although extracting, brewing, or ingesting them is probably unlawful.

    It is also extremely bad tasting, and almost invariably causes vomiting, hence the reference to such rituals as *la purga* (the purge) among native groups.

DATURA
(datura stramonium or datura inoxia)

Unlike simple psychedelics, datura is not the sort of plant that a casual occultist should bother using- much less an inexperienced or day tripping psychonaut.

A dangerously potent deliriant, datura is most often taken in the form of flower petal tea, or ground up and swallowed seeds (which taste slightly like black pepper.) However, the power of the plant is severe, bordering on the extreme, almost as potent a deliriant as nightshade (belladonna) or wolfsbane- both of which are also considered deliriants. This plant could have been listed in the prior section but its use as a mind altering species outweighs its use in the occult, strictly speaking, for other purposes.

The plant has a relatively long history of use- deliriants in general share this trait- for western tribes of the Americas were using the insanely powerful mescal bean before they found out that salvia was more fun and less toxic.

One tale tells of soldiers during the civil war who accidentally ate the plant's rather tasty looking pods, thinking they were edible- an entire brigade of them ended up stark naked wandering through the woods for two days, after which they recalled seeing Satan and demons repeatedly to their commanders (after which it was dubbed "thorn apple" or "devil's apple".) This anecdotal report, which might otherwise be overlooked, is very likely to be true- such are the effects of larger quantities of the plant. The seeds, pods, stems, leaves, and roots all contain hallucinogenic compounds, which are dangerous.

However, due to its relatively high toxicity, this particular plant should not be used unless the occultist wants to spend an extended period of time in an absorbing hallucination in which the physical and spiritual world essentially overlap- and in which the user may think they are sitting down in a chair, when really they are rolling around on the floor or running through the streets. The probability of death or arrest on datura is present and measurable.

It is, however, also capable of being used in smaller doses (40 to 50 seeds) in which the visual hallucinations tend to be weaker than with a higher dose. Within my own experimentation, I was able to encourage strange visual effects, in which arcane-looking script appeared before my eyes when they were closed, some of which appeared to be mathematical functions, and some of which seemed to be in Latin- which flashed before my eyes for extended periods- however, I then spent the better part of a day with thirst that water cannot quench (the salivary glands become compromised by its use.) It also has the strange ability to make very bland foods taste amazingly good while making flavorful foods taste like cardboard or sawdust.

It is a true spiritual substance; however, the danger of using it means I must mention it more for the sake of a completed list of such substances, rather than because I encourage others to use it. However, for those who insist upon using it, it is extremely easy to propagate, tends to spread around on its own, and is extremely inexpensive to purchase in even huge quantities. Like henbane, it will quickly attempt to invade areas surrounding its original propagation and the seeds must be stratified to germinate. This normally means sowing the seeds in autumn in cool climates, or refrigerating them in a warmer one where snow and frost is rare or absent.

FLY AGARIC
(amanita muscaria)

Fly agaric mushrooms, which grow throughout North America, Europe, and Asia, are one of the most stereotypical mind altering life forms on the planet. (It must be noted, however, that they are toxic to ingest even when prepared "properly.") It is the typical red mushroom with white spots, depicted in every *Super Mario* game. It won't make the user grow taller, but it may make them feel stronger.

Producing both muscimol and muscarine (in various percentages according to the region) they have been used for a long time particularly among Siberian groups- in a ritual which has changed quite strangely over time.

Originally, the Siberians would ingest the mushrooms directly, which caused nausea and delirium most of the time- so while it enabled them to commune with divine forces in their rituals, they eventually discovered that if reindeer ate the mushrooms, and they then drank the urine of the deer, that it removed most of the negative effects- eventually shaman cornered the market on the mushrooms and fulfilled the same urine-based role. I have briefly mentioned the procession of this form of occultism from *disorganized and familial* to *semi-organized* and finally *to the level of an organized cultist movement* in one of my other works; namely "Psychedelic Spirituality." This process mimics many other religious movements through the past of human history into the modern age.

The experience ranges from frightening to strange- mostly revolving around feeling weightless and energized, while light appears more bright than normal (leading some to argue that viking berserkers ingested the mushroom before battle- something which has not been verified and may be mere legend.) Delirium and confusion is common at higher doses. The normal cutoff dose is twelve grams. Up to that point, assuming "roughly average" muscimol content and proper preparation (drying of the caps) to remove muscarine, the psychedelic effects are notable and primary. After that dosage, at twelve grams or thereabouts, delirium, short or long lasting, gains dominance and overwhelms the effects of the muscimol.

Oddly, some woodcuts and art from the Medieval and Renaissance eras depict the tree of Eden in such a way that it resembles an *amanita* mushroom- these art pieces may have been informed by the presence of mushroom-using Gnostic cultists at the time. Either way, the imagery does appear to be meant literally.

While the fungi is not safe to ingest, and has caused at least a small number of fatalities to humans, it is still used to this day by the shaman in Asia (and probably elsewhere) for the same reason it was in ancient times- and the visions present at higher doses often lead to a deep sleep after several hours in which dreams are fantastically vivid and easily remembered, even for individuals who seldom encounter either state in their dreams. The mushrooms are generally legal unless ingested or extracted, and grow wild across much of Europe, Asia, and North America.

HAWAIIAN BABY WOODROSE
(argyreia nervosa)

    This rather strange plant, a tropical vine related peripherally to morning glory (also mentioned in this chapter) shares traits of both a psychedelic and deliriant nature, depending upon the style of use.

    Like morning glory, and like most plants listed, it has a long history behind it, particularly among the Central Americans (both ancient and modern!) as a means of seeing the world of spirits which the normal waking eye is not able to witness. Today, psychonauts, stoners, and Mesoamericans all use this same species, for perhaps vaguely different reasons.

Fruits of Eden, Herbalism and the Occult

Some individuals have seen Mayan-style pyramids and glowing beings walking around as though the spiritual world was physically overlain upon the "real" world while on this substance, but others have simply experienced nausea and delirium. The first alkaloids it contains (ergine and LSA) are merely LSD-related psychedelics of a weaker nature, which cause a meditative, trance-like state, along with encouraging visuals, but the outer coating of the seeds reportedly contain a deliriant which ought to be removed. In this process, the seeds are soaked before the outer coating is chipped away, or they may be sanded down. Reports of a specific deliriant in the seed coats are presumably true, although not yet fully verified.

Like morning glory, ergot, and related substances, the primary use of the chemicals in Hawaiian Baby Woodrose seem to be to encourage a relaxed state which borders upon forced meditation- and while eastern groups would shun the use of such substances, it is a fairly gentle, easy way for an individual to help train themselves into the states needed to go into full meditation (which is, of course, a mystic tradition.) The seeds also cause euphoria.

My own experience with this plant was largely negative and so morning glory seeds, for all their faults, were my preferred method of ergine ingestion, but most individuals (although I am not sure exactly why) prefer the woodrose method, possibly because it requires a far smaller amount of material be ingested. If cultivated, it is thus far easier.

There also seems to be a sort of animal spirit present in such substances- I have experienced, and others have experienced, a sort of urge to dance, sing, and draw pictures, while under its influence- a sort of tribal composite which almost makes one feel as though they have invoked some sort of spirit totem and are emulating an ancient pagan tribe. This species evokes Mesoamerican imagery, perhaps on a psychological, subconscious level.

As with any LSD relative, this substance can cause vasoconstriction and should not be used in dangerous doses, nor by individuals with heart or kidney problems, nor individuals with poor circulation of the blood- but (although they may exist) I have not heard of fatalities resulting from its use. It is generally legal unless ingested.

MORNING GLORY
(ipomoea tricolor)

Of all the plants listed in this section, morning glory is the one with which I have had the most experience- using it dozens of times and analyzing it quite frequently as a psychonaut.

Fruits of Eden, Herbalism and the Occult

Morning glory seeds contain similar compounds to Hawaiian Baby Woodrose- only without the deliriant outer seed coating, and a smaller percentage by weight, forcing the user to ingest a considerable (200 to 600 seed) quantity of fairly bad tasting material- ground up into powder as finely as possible.

It is my feeling that each substance contains a different style of spirit- and that an individual, for no real reason, may have either overwhelmingly good or bad experiences with particular substances simply because their own energies bind well with any of the substances listed (or unlisted.) And for myself, morning glory was the substance that tied in almost perfectly with my own spiritual beliefs and desires.

The experience is typically quite gentle, causing nausea often, but rarely vomiting, and a roughly 4 to 6 hour long "high" during which the main effects are a general feeling of laughter, relaxation, and colors becoming far brighter than normal- an overall effect which makes the user feel absolutely at ease, and even childlike, giggling or playing around in the dirt happily.

While some occultists may find this a bit too "happy" for their taste, and would rather munch down some wolfsbane to enter a berserker rage, the spiritual nature of this particular substance can be quite intoxicating- and while the user may not see spirits (like they may with salvia or ayahuasca brews) they will certainly feel spiritually connected, leading to a state in which ritualism becomes more spontaneous rather than planned, and during which state magick actually becomes far easier to use, unless the dosage was so high that the user becomes incoherent.

As children often are more in tune with magical properties than adults, perhaps we should look to the fairly common tale of a group of children passing around morning glory seeds in an attempt to "go to morning glory heaven." This often recounted story probably has a basis in reality- the entire experience tends to be quite positive, so long as a very high dose is avoided. With morning glory, most (presumably adult-involved) usages are anecdotally reported as negative or largely so. This seems out of step with "morning glory heaven" so often recounted and remarked upon by children or young adults. I theorize that the dose used by adults, often unremarkable stoners rather than actual psychonauts, is responsible.

Much like psilocybin, morning glory has two ways of deterring constant use- firstly, that after use, the individual is not physically able to enter such a state for a period of weeks or months (because the body becomes numbed to the chemicals involved) and secondly that the body, after the experience dies down, loses its craving for morning glory's effects for about the same period of time- the experience becomes self limiting, and the individual innately desires *not* to experience it again until these effects wear off. It is thus incapable of causing a physical addiction, although psychological habituation is of course still a possibility, even if remote.

As with Hawaiian Baby Woodrose, the warning about vasoconstriction still applies. The seeds are legal because they are cultivated widely, but LSA and ergine most likely fall under the drug analog act and ingesting the materials could result in prosecution.

OPIUM POPPY
(papaver somniferum)

Opium has an extremely long history of use all across Asia- along with hashish, being one of the primary mind altering substances of the region both among mystic groups and among the mainstream (albeit for different reasons.)

Although his own occult path is in question by some occult schools, one need look no further than Aleister Crowley, who was a fairly regular opium user, to see that some form of inspiration (whether truly spiritual or more philosophical) came to him from its use- and while ingesting opium is patently illegal in most parts of the world, the seeds to grow it are legal, and unless you attempt to grow a fairly large number of such plants (or to extract the resin from unripe pods to use it) it is normally overlooked by the legal system. In fact, the same seeds are used on baked goods every day without issue- a poppy seed bagel contains a very small amount of actual opium present in the seeds.

Opiates are predominantly a painkiller, but a decent dose of opium also causes visions, vivid and lucid dreams, and semi-hallucinatory states, and from a spiritual angle, it could be said that rather than thrusting the user headlong into a psychotic vision of dancing spirits, it instead allows them to passively observe the spiritual world from afar, without being unable to function normally- at least until they almost surely become addicted.

However, as this substance is both strictly illegal to ingest, as well as fairly addictive to use, it isn't something I can ethically encourage- while some individuals use it one in a while without issue, others end up seeking more and more of it, desperately craving its effects. Any heroin addict in the world has been addicted to a substance derived from these poppies.

Indeed, there have been groups whose existence revolves around the use of opiates or similar drugs in Asia for centuries- some have even gone so far as to mix cobra venom with their drugs, in an extreme show of fanaticism, although whether hashish or opium were originally used, is not entirely clear. This is "probably" dangerous.

At the very least, semi-refined opium in its organic state is probably less harmful and addictive than some of the refined products made from it (heroin and morphine in particular) and there are of course spiritual and occult paths who would shun the latter for its partially artificial makeup, while they may invite the use of opium in its primary form simply because it is organic (and the debate continues over whether this mindset is truly sensible.)

I cannot lay claim to having used opium, having decided against it due to the unfortunate addictive nature of the substance, but those who have, who I have spoken to, claim it is quite spiritual, and since it has been used for such purposes by others in the past, it is still worth listing. Some claim it is less addictive than usually suggested. I dispute this claim based on my personal interaction with those who have been addicted to such things.

PASSIONFLOWER
(passiflora edulis)

Passionflower is a stunning plant- with large, bright, lacy flowers which look like something from a jungle adventure movie.

Fruits of Eden, Herbalism and the Occult

Its beautiful appearance is only rivaled by its effects- which are heavily praised in the community of herbal medicine as a sleep aid for its quite powerful sedative effects. I have used both the plant itself, its fruit, and sleeping pills with its extract. The first two are more gentle, but the extract is potent.

It does work for this purpose- even some of the more fruity yogurts containing passionflower flesh and seeds will cause drowsiness, while eating an entire fruit will likely force you to take a nap- but it is what happens during these naps that allows it to be listed as a spiritually significant substance.

Firstly, sleeping under the effects of passionflower almost invariably cause vivid dreams- often with a strangely spiritual feeling to them- something which herbal science largely ignores in the attempt to look "legitimate" to the medical community.

Secondly, these dreams are also often lucid- I have had problems for years with experiencing lucid dreams (something which everyone seems obsessed with these days) but passionflower largely solves this problem, giving about a 50/50 chance of being able to control them- whether for astral purposes, or for your own fantasy entertainment. This was almost unheard of for me when I wasn't using *passiflora* extract in pill form.

Passionflower also makes meditation far easier- it calms the mind and can perhaps be combined with caffeine to create a state in which the individual is both able to focus and able to relax more easily (although I have not experimented with this method yet.)

Altogether, because the plant is not addictive, because it is generally considered safe in easy to consume doses, and because it is fairly easy to propagate (although it is a subtropical plant and will only grow indoors in most parts of the world) it is an excellent one for those wishing to work with meditation, yoga, and similar systems- although other plants such as valerian (the roots of valerian have similar effects) have been used by other groups of people for essentially the same purpose.

Passionflower has the additional bonus of being one of the few spiritually useful plants in which the part of the plant consumed for its effects is not of bad flavor or scent- in fact passionflower has a sweet, inviting scent, and an extremely well regarded taste, which is similar to, but more concentrated than, the flavor of a mango. The plant and its fruit and extracts are legal and commonly sold.

PSILOCYBIN
(Psilocybe and Panaeolus sp.)

Fruits of Eden, Herbalism and the Occult

It should be noted that even possessing psilocybin mushrooms is illegal- because the chemicals present are, themselves, controlled.

Psilocybin is one of the true psychedelics on this list, with effects that are similar to (but not quite identical to) any of the LSD family substances.

Mushrooms containing the active ingredient (psilocin) are found across much of the known world, although in warmer, wetter climates they tend to be more common- and like mescaline they are a sacrament to certain native tribes and nearly as important in their ritualism. Contrary to some conceptions of psilocybin as a "safe" psychedelic, it actually does have an achievable lethal dosage, although like a small number of other substances, the body tends to stop "wanting" to ingest it after one or two uses, for a period of some weeks or months. It is thus self limiting as is morning glory, generally speaking.

Psilocybin tends to cause objects to melt into one another in a bright show of psychedelic colors- and its ability to cause literal hallucinations may have led to its identification with animal totems and rituals involved with communicating with them. During my own use of a particularly potent strain of *Azurescens* caps, (which look like alien food, colored pale ashen blue,) I found myself simultaneously inside a cathedral made of crystal and dew drops, and above a sea of gelatin, pulsing up and down and changing colors.

Mayans and Aztecs were both known to have ingested psilocin containing species of fungi- in order to communicate with their elaborate pantheons of deities.

Unlike with other substances, psilocybe containing species seem to quite commonly create a spiritual experience. With many psychedelic or similar substances, an individual *may experience* cosmic forces, and in some cases this depends on their own outlook on reality- but with psilocybin, even people not taking part in specific ritualism sometimes report a cosmic experience. Even those who do not think deeply about spirituality tend to see such strange things on these species of mushroom, that it may open their eyes to the spiritual world, even against their will.

Feeling connected to the world itself and to otherwise unseen forces which become tangible on psilocybin mushrooms is also fairly common- and as with ayahuasca, DMT, and their uncannily common capability to evoke the presence of creative orbs of light, psilocybin seems to share the tendency to have surprisingly similar stereotypical effects in a wide range of individuals.

Fruits of Eden, Herbalism and the Occult

SALVIA DIVINORUM
(salvia divinorum)

Among all the plants listed in this chapter, salvia divinorum is one of the strangest and most blatantly spiritual plants of all. I have no idea, myself, why it is so generally overlooked by psychonauts, warded off as it were by mostly negative reports regarding its effects.

Commonly used by Central American natives, this substance appears to have replaced the highly toxic and dangerously powerful mescal bean in spiritual use some time ago- and while news reports in the mid 2000s played up how dangerous this substance is, it seems to have been largely overblown and misunderstood in nature, with most reported fatalities either dubious, or obviously fabricated- some were even borrowed from the late 1960s utterly, and merely recycled by the media as though these drug war tales were true.

With this plant, properly used, it is possible to transcend directly into the astral plane for short periods of time- a potency which goes, in my opinion, even beyond DMT or ayahuasca, into the realm of what may be the most powerful drug mankind has at his disposal. I say this of course, to denote its spiritual usage, not its entertainment value, or its medicinal action.

Typically smoked in semi-extracted form (in which extracted salvinorin is re-incorporated into additional dried salvia leaves) the experience tends to last a very short time, typically under 15 minutes (a trait shared by purified DMT!) but is intense and sometimes difficult to comprehend. Like with morning glory, I believe that the plurality of "bad trips" involved with salvia relate to people thinking they need to imbibe more of it than they actually do, especially if it is their first time using it.

It may make reality become fractal, such that the individual blacks out for several minutes and then becomes conscious, as reality slowly spins to a halt and returns to normal. While experimenting with salvia, I once had sex (literally and physically) with a woman that materialized from my bed- and slowly appeared in front of me (some may refer to this as a succubus.) On salvia, oddly, this sort of experience is relatively normal, or at least it was for me; others seem often at a loss to explain what they saw beyond a "tornado of color" or "spinning nothingness."

The world around the user tends to change form- not in the manner of LSD or mushrooms in which things change size and flash in different colors, but that objects literally appear to converge with one another, forming new objects, sometimes forming a sort of "story" in the mind of a user, which ranges from frightening to extremely pleasurable. The first use of salvia, or the first time using a higher dose than before, tends to be slightly disturbing, with subsequent uses typically more gentle.

The use of meditative music while using salvia seems to invite additional strange experiences, in which objects begin to disintegrate into smoke, or where music "melts" into reality, and changes wildly from that which is actually playing.

While salvia has been labeled dangerous and been outlawed in some parts of the world, I do not personally believe the wild stories given as to fatalities from its use- as they closely resemble similar (and debunked) stories regarding LSD from the 1960s and cannabis from the 1930s reefer madness period, however as with any substance, dosage should be considered, and caution exercised. It is now, unfortunately, illegal in most US states and most nations, although it is still sold on the internet from areas where it is legal.

SAN PEDRO
(trichocereus pahanoi/ trichocereus sp.)

Peyote, which has been used for many centuries by Native Americans, grows wild across the western United States, but is outlawed except for "authentic" natives to use; a rather discriminatory policy circa the early drug war- however, several species of cacti containing the same chemicals albeit in smaller amounts, are perfectly legal to buy, sell, and grow (although technically not to use.) I could expound on the problems and inconsistencies behind the western drug war for a hundred pages here but won't- those who want to hear my views on those subjects can read my other works on psychedelia.

Fruits of Eden, Herbalism and the Occult

San Pedro cactus is quite common in landscaping for dry, hot areas of North America- and as such is widely available for growing purposes- and its spiritual nature is very much the same as the more potent-by-weight peyote, containing mescaline. I have seen landscaping cacti in Texas; San Pedro was among the most common for such street-side decor.

Typically crushed as finely as possible and either extracted into "cactus juice" or mixed with acidic compounds to release the mescaline (such as lemon juice) and then consumed, mescaline from San Pedro is a very powerful psychedelic, the effects of which almost remind the user of the deserts where it grows naturally. It tends to cause waves of cool and warm down the spine, with a slight massage sensation along the same area; it also tends to cause objects to seem detached from reality, in such a state that they appear to float away like clouds.

The sort of shamanistic desert spirits informing this substance are quite profound- and while I didn't see lizard men riding vultures while under its effects, the physical sensations were extremely relaxing, and the visual effects stunning, giving an appreciation of nature.

Interestingly, peyote rituals are still conducted frequently by native tribes- giving a fairly obvious allusion to its spiritual usefulness. Mescaline cacti are also easily grown, although raids by the government on growers are fairly frequent, even when no proof exists that they were meant for consumption.

It may be worth noting that everyone's favorite outlaw shaman, Charles Manson, was quite well versed in the use of both mescaline and psilocybin from his time spent among certain native groups- but while some may consider Manson a criminal psychotic, one can divorce his spiritualism from these connotations and clearly draw a connection between his advocacy for nature and naturism, and his many hours spent under the influence of cacti and mushrooms. When you observe his frequent allusions to Abraxas and reflections, one can see that he has had perhaps more training in at least Gnosticism than most give him credit for.

While San Pedro and similar species are wonderful substances, they are illegal to ingest, and thus care must be taken if use is determined to be desirable for occult purposes.

WILD OPIUM LETTUCE
(lactuca virosa)

An extremely common (and even noxious) weed that grows across most of North America's temperate zones, lactuca virosa was originally considered a possible hoax until it was discovered that claims of its mind altering nature were true (something I have experimented with firsthand.)

Typically, in an interesting extraction method, the unripe pods are picked before they flower, and then heated on tin foil to create a thick resin which is then smoked, creating a mild sedative effect and an almost marijuana-like effect (closer to mostly indica than to mostly sativa blends.)

Thankfully, because the plant and its compounds are not scheduled substances, its use is (at the time of writing this) completely legal, and is used occasionally for headaches as well on a medicinal level.

While I am not sure it has any documented spiritual use, (tribal individuals probably didn't have any reason to extract its resin for use when they already had mushrooms and such,) it may have been previously used for medicinal purposes, as some suggest the plant can be made into a tea as well as extracted to smoke. Despite the name opium lettuce, it contains no opiates or opioids. A similar species, *Lactuca serriola*, has some similar uses but is not considered as potent; at least according to the anecdotal accounts I am privy to. I have used virosa, although only sporadically, but serriola I never cultivated.

Because the effects are said to fairly closely mimic marijuana, I suggest that it is a suitable replacement for it for spiritual purposes- since marijuana is, of course, illegal in most parts of the world due to its usefulness in making cheap, renewable paper products- and I have not personally heard of any negative effects of its use, although it's entirely possible some individuals may be allergic to its pollen as with any other plant. I didn't notice it as being similar to most marijuana strains I ever ingested- it was relaxing yes, and a mild euphoriant, but causes effects not particularly similar to more than a tiny amount of cannabis.

This plant, as mentioned, grows wild in many places, but those who wish to cultivate it will not find it hard to purchase the seeds to do so, and the growth rate of the plant is quite high, considering it is used to poor soil and crowded, recently disrupted environments in which nutrients are scant at best. The seeds can be autumn-sown in any cleared or mostly cleared plot, even a piece of marginal land by a roadside, and simply left there to come up on their own, and they will still thrive. If they are fertilized and cared for, they become even more massive.

It may be a good compliment to other substances which may cause hallucinations- sometimes, a mild sedative like lactuca virosa, valerian, or passionflower is used in conjunction in order to calm the mind and body or to stave off negative thoughts or reactions, in the hope that it will create a far more positive overall experience, but even taken alone, wild opium lettuce is potent enough for mention. I can legally give no advice here on drug interactions when using it in tandem with other substances nor do I thus recommend doing so.

WORMWOOD
(artemisia absinthium)

This often overlooked little relative of common wormwood (mugwort) is one of the most fascinating and spiritually related plants of all time. It is the main ingredient in flavoring absinthe, and giving it its psychedelic reputation. Modern absinthe blends, especially those in the USA, tend to contain little or even no thujone derived from little or even no Absinthe wormwood.

Not normally present in large enough amounts in absinthe to cause a full blown psychedelic effect (but appearing often in large enough quantities to create a borderline, pre-psychedelic state) thujone, the active ingredient in this type of wormwood, is indeed a psychedelic (and has killed people who attempted to ingest large quantities of the extracted substance) and causes psychedelic effects which run a strange line between opiates and true psychedelics like mescaline or LSD. It is very dangerous to meddle with extracted thujone, although the plants themselves are relatively benign and mostly decorative unless absinthe is being made.

The "green fairy" was implicated in the Victorian era as causing vivid hallucinations, opiate-like stupor, and sometimes violence- however it seems that this was due more to the extreme alcohol content of absinthe and not the presence of a fairly small amount of thujone- absinthe is more alcoholic than most liquors, rivaling or surpassing some of the more potent gin and whiskey on the market- and due to the typical ingestion method which involves sugaring it with a special spoon, it may be that some people simply drank themselves into a trance and went ballistic, not realizing it was far more alcoholic than the wine most people of the period were used to.

However, thujone is a spiritually useful substance, and some of the Victorian era occultism seems to have been affected by the use of absinthe- a trait shared by some of the non-spiritual literature of the time period. When we observe art from the surrealist period we're sometimes observing the effects of absinthe and thus thujone, on these works.

I have ingested thujone for its bizarre effects, but I have not used absinthe (which is both expensive and hard to find in smaller stores.) And it does cause a strange effect, which seems to be sedative, painkiller, and mild psychedelic at the same time. It is, however, not particularly impressive when compared to mescaline or amanita mushrooms, and it is not as enjoyable and "clean" an experience as morning glory, so I never dabbled with it beyond a cursory experimentation.

The green fairy is even alluded to in Bram Stoker's *Dracula* and seems to have played some role in conceptions of vampirism- as both spiritualistic and romantic, seen as a gateway to other realms of thought, or even other worlds- although thujone's power is debatable for such purposes. Mostly, when we discuss the topic, we have to divorce actual *thujone* experimentation from anything involving absinthe itself, where it may just be the alcohol causing any noted effects. Further, the legend surrounding absinthe- even largely thujone-free modern absinthe, continues to cause people to think of it as a drug rather than just alcohol as they may regard whiskey or gin, and this has a deep and profound effect upon the experience they thus have. This facet of absinthe muddies the waters with regards to documenting its actual spiritual qualities.

It does bear listing, however, because of both the cultural significance of the use of absinthe and its plant compounds, as well as its very real psychedelic nature, assuming it does contain a substantial enough percentage of wormwood-derived thujone to actually be a psychedelic.

This plant is a close relative of mugwort and is virtually indistinguishable from it. For the illustration, therefore, refer to mugwort. (page 67-69.)

CHAPTER FIVE
Plants used in love-related occult rituals

BARLEY
(hordeum vulgare)

Barley is inextricably linked to the topic of love (and lust) in folk tradition, partially because of its similarities to other cereal grains and thus ability to cultivate ergot fungus, which itself has a long tradition of interfering with human culture in social manners. Even more, as a staple crop for thousands of years, it is necessarily linked to harvest rituals, and thus fertility rites.

Barley, as a strictly agricultural grain, is not generally grown except as an ornamental by gardeners unless they have a field to devote to actual farming- but barley stalks can be purchased nonetheless for decorative purposes. One of the first domesticated crops, barley was seen as a source and symbol of abundance in Europe and Asia, and linked to the early production of alcoholic drinks (which also are tied to- sometimes misbegotten- lust.) It tends to grow with relative ease on moderately fertile soil.

The growth of ergot on barley and other cereal grains seems to have a significant cultural tie to its use as a symbol of lust and fertility- for the ingestion of the toxic ergot fungus in infected grain causes strange, aberrant, confused behavior and may have easily led to the infected person experiencing psychotic levels of sexual desire. When we reckon with the Salem Witch Trials (perhaps a less positive grain-related period in history) we are witnessing, most likely, the result of ergotamine poisoning courtesy of rye or barley.

Barley is often also used for harvest-season decoration. A

pleasant looking grain, it will last for some time when dried and hung, and is thought to bring youth and vigor into a home. This is straight from the harvest/fertility rite traditions of Europe.

It has additional, more medicinal uses- for a wash made by simply steeping barley heads in water is supposed in some new age circles to protect the youthful appearance of the skin, while it can also be made into a tea when roasted (which is supposedly of good flavor.) Since it presumably contains collagen, its use as a facial wash to stave off wrinkles is probably based in reality.

If barley is to be grown in any significant quantity, and the gardener wishes to remain organic and not make use of fertilizer, it will be necessary to alternate crops of barley with crops of legumes (beans, peas, and so forth) in order to maintain a balance of nitrogen in the soil, which will be leeched by the grain if it is repeatedly grown alone- this is referred to as crop rotation (and also helps suppress the growth of ergot which, while culturally significant, is toxic and very bad to ingest.) It can also be companion planted with peas or beans when it is grown, infusing even more nitrogen into the plant roots.

Barley cakes have also been used in divinatory processes (alphinomancy) in which those suspected of a crime were made to eat barley cakes, and the guilty individual(s) were supposed to experience intestinal discomfort, while all other partakers would remain unscathed. It is not known how many were used in these "trials"- one would expect such a compacted grain cake to be gastro-intestinally unsettling to most people partaking as such.

BLEEDING HEART
(lamprocapnos spectabilis)

The bleeding heart plant is almost innately referred to in love-related magick, possessing branching stems which hold a multitude of exactly heart shaped, pink and white blossoms- it is easily grown in some areas, but sometimes rejects soil for seemingly no reason. Its flower shape makes it a rather obvious candidate for those using them in love related spellwork.

The plant is linked to several folk tales- one from Japan in which its existence is explained by a certain young man who failed to win the love of his crush, and another folk tale from the Americas (possibly Europe beforehand) in which it is said that to divine whether the one you love returns your affection, you crush one of the flowers, and it if "bleeds" the return of your love by your beloved is assured. The flowers do not actually bleed their color readily so the rejection rate for those using such an off-hand ritual was probably high.

The plant cannot be ingested or used in incense (having very little fragrance) and so to make use of it for love rituals, its heart shaped flowers are most often strewn about an altar- or else kept in ones' pocket, a satchel, or under ones' pillow. When dried they roughly retain their shape, but become withered, losing some of their luster. These little dried flower shells, as they tend to appear, are extremely light and when powdered result in a tiny amount of material only.

The flowers can also be crushed after drying, into a powder, and this powder sprinkled on a belonging of the one you wish to have love for you- It is not certain where this tale originates, but I have heard of it in New England, so it likely has either British or Welsh roots. In some variants, it is mixed with crushed morning glory petals, which of course would have been added within the context of the Americas themselves, being native to these subtropical regions rather than the temperate forests of the old world.

The seeds of the bleeding heart plant may be used as well- they are kept, simply, in a jar or a bowl, and used as a symbol of love about to blossom in the coming year- these seeds are then ritualistically planted, with good growth indicating the fast coming of love into ones' life. The rhizomes (bulb-like roots) of the plant can also be used in a similar manner- the plant actually grows more easily from a rhizome than from the seeds, some of which tend to be sterile, and some of which tend to die as seedlings.

The plant is also a favorite of certain types of butterflies and other beneficial pollinating insect life- having a small patch of bleeding heart will draw positive energy to a location. The attraction of pollinators helps ensure fertility not just to the one plant itself, or the patch of bleeding hearts, but rather to the entire garden. This important strategy in agricultural workings is overlooked by some.

CATNIP
(nepeta cataria)

    Catnip is at first only obviously connected with driving felines berserk- but it is actually edible in tea, and has mild sedative or stimulant effects on humans, as well as a spiritual usefulness in rituals related to love and physical vigor. Extremely easily grown, and self-spreading, catnip can achieve magnificent heights fairly quickly and may quickly colonize the marginal areas of a garden. More than an herb as it is commonly considered, it forms a massive growth of long stems which more closely resembles a small bush, sometimes five to six feet high if the soil is choice and the plant's area kept free of weeds.

For women, it is said to make them more alluring (and, considering it stimulates humans in a similar manner that it does cats, this may be a very real chemical action.) It is most often extracted and used as a sort of perfume, or else taken in a tea, or simply rubbed on the skin, which is also invigorating and feels "minty." It leaves a cool feeling on the flesh when crushed and applied.

Tea simply made from dried catnip leaves is a mild sedative similar to chamomile and amusingly similar in flavor as well. It is entirely edible and has been used in folk medicine to improve vigor for some time.

Smoking catnip (as in, through a pipe) gives a roughly opposite effect to the sedation of drinking it as an herbal tea- much like a cat will be strongly stimulated by smelling a catnip plant, only to eat it and then fall asleep, it has a very similar although dulled action on humans, being not as strong for humans as for cats in either of its actions. When ingested, thus, it is a mild sedative, and when smoked, a mild stimulant of some kind.

Catnip can also be burned in conjunction with incense, which is supposed to make the effect and the scent more mild- this is noted as having the most beneficial effect when used with incense or other implements designed to capture love or increase physical lust. It is possible that rituals involving such use date to the times of literal feline worship, circa antiquity.

Oddly, some cats react to valerian the same way they do to catnip- which is odd only because both catnip and valerian have been used as a sedative tea for human consumption for some time. Some folk tales suggest that catnip roots are the strongest, most medicinally and spiritually active segment of the plant, although the leaves (and sometimes buds and flowers) are most commonly used. The flowers, if picked before going to seed, can be kept in the pocket to encourage members of the opposite sex to be attracted to the one bearing them. The scent is most potent if the plants are trimmed and the trimmings thus harvested in late summer, especially when weather is dry following a day or two of good rain. Thinner soils produce more scent in the plants also, and they coexist well with basil.

Catnip tea can be made by also adding dried lavender and honey to the mix, which is supposed to potentiate its chemical action as well as making it far more fragrant- while lavender is more a protective herb than a love-inducing herb, they combine well and this is a typical way to take it as herbal tea. Honey, when added as such, can also be seen here as being involved with love or lust- it has its own ancient usage as an apparently effective vaginal treatment to prevent pregnancy before intercourse.

COLUMBINE
(aquilegia sp.)

Columbine flowers are one of the more showy, potent symbols of love in the botanical world. It is fairly difficult to propagate from seed, but easy to grow from its perennial roots in all cool and temperate climates (especially in higher elevations.) My own plantings have been mostly but not completely unsuccessful.

Columbines are easily used in several manners, but the most common manner is simply to get a growth of the flowers started, and then surreptitiously plant one of the perennial roots onto the property of the person that is to be affected by such ritualism. (Although this is technically in a legal gray area, it is doubtful that most people would object to someone planting a columbine in their garden.)

It can also be used in conjunction with invocations and love spells- simply by placing the dried flowers, the wet cuttings, or a whole, potted plant onto the altar, or near the altar, or near the ritual space, which is supposed to infuse the area with lustful energy. The sexually colored plants are as bright as can be, and their symbology thus easily explained and understood.

Simply growing columbines is said to increase the likelihood of meeting an available and suitable partner. They are extremely attractive and will spread with ease especially on a sloping garden on the side of a hill or in terrain which is mountainous, where thin soil may make growing other plants difficult in some areas.

The flowers of the columbine plant are claimed to be edible- they are sometimes consumed in folk ritual to increase the sexual virility or attractiveness of a man to a woman (although other parts of the plant are said to be toxic.) I cannot vouch for their flavor or the safety of ingesting them; they may contain any of a number of toxic compounds, causing acute problems or problems if ingestion is prolonged.

In some ways, the more showy a flower is, the more it tends to be linked to lust, love, and ritualism revolving around fertility. Linked to the goddess Venus, columbine is no exception to this facet of ritualism- for its bright and normally multicolored blossoms may indeed win over the hearts of those they are given to (for even simply giving a pretty girl flowers is, almost, itself a ritual, with deep cultural connections and rites associated with it, especially of the behavioral sort.)

Some variants of the columbine flower grow wild throughout the world, but are endangered or threatened, and thus care should be taken to identify the specific variant before attempting to pick or take root cuttings from any species found in the wold.

DAFFODIL
(narcissus sp.)

Daffodil is linked to two cultures, in each linked with a historic use in mysticism (and in medicine, although ingestion of the plant is a bad idea due to its nauseating qualities.) Easily grown from its prolific bulbs, it is a common sight in spring gardens. There is no more common spring time flower in the northern climates, other than perhaps the tulip.

In the East, which less concerns its use as a mystical bringer of love, the narcissus or daffodil is used variously for celebrations of New Years' in which its possession and growth is said to increase wealth- but it is also used in certain poultices and balms which are used in these same Eastern cultures, to drive toxins out of the body. The bulbs contain certain oily substances used for this purpose when crushed and macerated.

In the more regularly regarded western tradition, daffodils (perhaps because they are often the first flower to bloom come the spring thaw, other than the crocus or snowdrop lily,) are seen as a powerful symbol of vitality and birth, and of course, along with this, of fertility and love. The bulbs themselves are sometimes used in rituals, while the flowers, when grown or when cut and used to decorate the home, are thought to increase the chances of getting lucky in a relationship.

Commonly, the bulb is kept as a sort of amulet, worn on a string or allowed to rest in the pocket of one who intends to begin a relationship, or who wishes for a relationship to come to them- the use of a daffodil bulb as a sort of amulet seems most common in the mountainous northeast United States, and the tradition may have come from English or French heritage as colonization began. It is common here in northern Appalachia.

Fruits of Eden, Herbalism and the Occult

Although it is not certain that this narcissus is the one mentioned in Greek literature, it has connotations which link it to the tale of Narcissus himself, whose own personal beauty and vanity was so great that he stared at his reflection until he succumbed and died- the daffodil, of the same name, is thus used as a symbol of beauty, although it has no medicinal application in restoring it. In this odd story, the protagonist has the love he desires already, but ends up enchanted by his *own* physical beauty- likely a statement about vanity and its destructive abilities.

It has been suggested (notably by Pliny the Elder) that the plant was a type of mind altering drug, although such beliefs may be more the result of poisoning from its ingestion, or of misidentification, than its actual usefulness as a drug. I have heard of no study which resolves the issue in favor of classing the daffodil as a mind altering species. I theorize that this is merely the result of its noxious contents, in a manner similar to the use of strychnine (a deadly poison) in small, sub-lethal quantities to mimic LSD, or so it is said, when cut with actual drugs, to save on drug manufacturing costs.

The bulbs can also be used to represent human souls, and incantations said over them, in order to attempt to cause a person to lust after the occultist- simply by creating a suitable ritual for doing so. Like with other fleshy roots, bulbs, and so forth, symbols can be carved in the daffodil bulb in sigil form, for which they could be used for various purposes.

DEVIL'S PAINTBRUSH
(pilosella aurantiaca)

Often, a plant called "indian paintbrush" is referred to in folk tales as a love-inducing and charming garden staple, with such tales centered around Northern Appalachia, where it is considered lucky to take wild specimens and cultivate them- or else to fashion the stems and flowers into bracelets. These tales are sometimes misconstrued, with the more western, real Indian Paintbrush being medicinal (and spiritually important to Native Americans) yet not the same plant that those in the Northeast refer to as "indian paintbrush."

Fruits of Eden, Herbalism and the Occult

The devil's paintbrush is the indian paint brush of the Northeast- it is a vaguely dandelion-looking but orange plant also called orange hawkweed- an invasive species originally from Europe.

Local folk tales in the region prescribe that the stem and flower should be plucked, and then these formed into a type of bracelet- with the goal of obtaining love. Two people who have found love in this manner, then twine the two bracelets together, in hope that this will help them to maintain it. This binding together of the two people involved is centuries old.

The plant seems to have limited benefit in herbal medicine, with its sole recognized use being in applying the macerated leaves and/or stems to a wound in order to help keep it closed and prevent it from festering. Cultivating hawkweed is simple, as it is largely a weed escaped from colonial gardens, and will grow in most soils and slowly take over patches of lawn where it is not removed. Seeds or roots can be used to plant it.

It is considered good luck to care for devil's paintbrush plants- it is thought that watering them or creating a space for them to colonize will bring love and warmth to the home- however, the plants will likely move in invited or uninvited, and are difficult to suppress.

It should be noted that in some states and in some provinces of Canada, the plant is illegal to actively cultivate due to its noxious weed status- additionally, it is considered to be toxic for horses and certain other livestock to ingest (although it isn't listed as explicitly toxic for humans.)

Having documented as much Appalachian lore as I can, I believe that the switch from calling this species "devil's paintbrush" (its authentic title) to "indian paintbrush" thus confusing it with *castilleja* was partially a result of the Satanic Panic, during which time (roughly beginning in the early 1980s) even mentioning the word "devil" was feared and considered of ill omen.

INDIAN PAINTBRUSH
(castilleja sp.)

The true Indian Paintbrush which grows largely in the Western regions of North America is considered quite the beneficial herb- used by native tribes for centuries before colonial contact, and thereafter equally made use of by the colonists. It seems to prefer drier climates, especially those in hilly or mountainous regions, and would be difficult to propagate in wet areas.

Like the devil's paintbrush, indian paintbrush plants are seen as particularly useful in obtaining love- there are two methods by which it is used, the first being to take possession of some of the plants' petals and keep them on the person (in the pocket, or in a satchel) and the second being to steep the flowering parts of the plant in hot water, and using the mixture as a body wash whilst bathing- both methods are thought to improve personal attractiveness.

With yet another link to sexual and romantic functions, the plant was thought (perhaps in a valid way) to be useful in treating sexual diseases by the Natives- its high selenium content may actually have made it of some use in doing so- and the flowering parts of the plant are (in small quantities) still eaten from time to time, although the stems and roots are toxic.

In a tip of the hat to its own name, the indian paintbrush does not merely resemble a paintbrush literally, but can be used to produce a variety of colorful dyes- something which it does not share with its eastern cousin hawksweed. The two species are easily differentiated.

A wash made from this plant may be used to prevent baldness when used to cleanse the hair (along with its use as a body wash.) Its purported ability to do so may connect it further to increasing and maintaining a level of attractiveness to the opposite sex.

It is said that the origin of the plant (according to native tradition) involves a certain artist who was gifted a variety of colorful brushes by the great spirit when his attempt to replicate nature scenes was unsuccessful with the mere use of war paint and that, upon discarding each brush, it was turned into a different color of this same plant. It has seen heavy use in native medicine and culture, and has been further used by those who first encountered native culture.

MISTLETOE
(viscum album)

An over-harvested and now regrettably fairly uncommon wild plant in Europe, mistletoe is a strange parasitic herb which requires a host tree in order to grow- as such it can be fairly difficult to cultivate, because although seeds are available and the method is fairly simple, getting it to take hold is hit and miss.

Mistletoe is often seen as the stereotypical Christmas plant (although it is amusingly often represented by Holly instead which has red rather than white berries.) The use of mistletoe in kissing rituals has roots in the pagan medicinal use of the plant as a contraceptive following wintertime orgiastic rituals- and it was considered sacred (both for purely ritualistic, and for medicinal use) by the druids.

In what modern christians insist is coincidence, mistletoe was connected to the festival of Saturnalia in Roman times (the festival which led most directly to almost every Christmas tradition at later dates) and would later be used almost identically by those same christians. There is a long-standing pagan tradition that the days of pre-christian glory would begin anew shortly after mistletoe crossed the threshold of a christian church. Bringing mistletoe into churches was thus outlawed in the early christian era, and this ban continued for centuries. The age of christianity, according to this prophecy, began its downfall roughly at the end of the Satanic Panic when wiccans managed to bring mistletoe, for the first time, into a church in Europe. Perhaps this is why the first pagan temple to be built in Europe in centuries is being constructed in Iceland right now.

The powdered leaves of mistletoe may be mixed with powdered verbena in some new age mixtures, as a form of love powder, which is supposed to be sprinkled first upon the self, and then surreptitiously upon the individual desired- it is also mixed with charred and powdered oak as a hex breaker, which may have its origin in the druid tradition of mistletoe harvested from oak trees (which is uncommon due to the thickness of its bark) being of particular importance.

Hanging mistletoe in the home is considered exceptionally protective- first and foremost preventing the home from catching fire or being struck by lightning, and secondly to prevent discord and promote peace and love in the home.

Like other medicinally and spiritually active plants, the medieval church attempted (and failed) to ban mistletoe and drive it to extinction, in the belief that its effects upon fertility and usefulness within lust driven ritualism was demonic. This attempted suppression of mankind by reducing its will to mate was never apparently viable

Fruits of Eden, Herbalism and the Occult

and was ignored by the laity.

The wood of mistletoe can be used to fashion wands and amulets- but it should be privately cultivated for this purpose, as it is a fairly uncommon plant (especially outside of Europe) and has repeatedly been driven towards extinction, first by the church and then by woodsmen who felt it was a threat to the trees which it colonized parasitically.

RADISH
(raphanus sativus)

The common radish, which might be the most easily grown plant aside from the common string bean, is assuredly occult in nature, possessing powerful medicinal qualities, as well as having a more directly physical use within the occult, herbalist realm. Most people don't know this, though, since it's mostly used as a salad topping.

Radish is seen in several cultures as extremely good at enhancing the male sexual drive- it is commonly consumed in large quantities in Appalachia, as well as Japan, for this purpose- although the powerful flavor of the radish (horseradish, while unrelated, is used for the same purpose in the Eastern mountains of the USA!) means that some will suffer attempting to use it in this way.

Pliny mentions radishes as being able to prevent scorpions from stinging- while it is not recommended to test this hypothesis, the acrid vapors that radish juice releases might actually repel some types of animals.

The other occult use of the radish is due to its rather woody composition when it ages (younger radishes are considered better tasting, so older radishes are either allowed to go to seed, or get thrown out, most commonly.) Here in New England, I have heard of people carving the name of someone they wish to go out with, onto an older, woody radish, and burying it on the other person's property, or using various folk incantations with similar methods. This slightly amusing radish symbolism appears to extend at least halfway down the Appalachian chain into the West Virginia area and perhaps further.

Radishes also seem to have been carved into amulets and worn around the neck or kept in the pocket in the same region, for the same purpose as eating it; to increase and maintain virility and to increase the individual's ability to find a suitable partner.

Fruits of Eden, Herbalism and the Occult

The rather volatile scent of radish (and unrelated horseradish) juices, have been used to clear up congestion as well whether the result of flu or cold- a few good whiffs of either will cause the nasal passages to empty rapidly, and I can attest to this being extremely effective- the topical use of its juice on the skin to clear it up is, however, ineffective. Macerated, partially liquefied radish root may be used to clean wounds and prevent them from becoming foul- and it seems to have some level of antibacterial action of some sort.

Radish may have been first identified as tied to lust and fertility by its purported ability to cause mothers to increase lactation- it also has been said to encourage menstruation.

THYME
(thymus vulgaris)

Thyme is considered important in the practice of love magick. A relatively small plant, it will come back year after year in warmer climates, but is grown as an annual in Northern regions. It thrives in rich soils.

Thyme is thought to be of particular usefulness for females who wish to attract a man (although it does work in reverse as well.) It is also used in rituals intended to get over lost love and find new love- usually this is done by taking a fragrant bath steeped with thyme, although it can also be kept on the body.

It can also be made into a smudge (in the manner of white sage) and used in this dried, bundled form to destroy negativity and attract love to the home- it is less often used in this way, but it functions very much as an incense, and is quite pungent. It may also be used simply to attract pollinators to the garden, which then improve all other plants in the area.

A tea made from steeping thyme sprigs in hot water can be used both for medicinal purposes (usually curing a stubborn cough) as well as to purify the skin- oils found in thyme are mildly antimicrobial, and thus washing with the cooled tea product can help to clear up the skin- the most natural way to make oneself more attractive to a lover.

When simply grown in the garden, thyme is attractive towards positive energies, and defends against negative ones- it has been implicated also in use for exorcism and banishing or repulsing evil spirits- normally in order to use it for this purpose, it is either used in a smudge, or else kept fresh on or near the altar when rituals are being performed.

Thyme is best used for ritual purposes (if it is to be burned or used as a sort of herbal offering) when combined with dragons' blood (which increases its potency) and rosemary (which increases its positive qualities.)

It is said that thyme will also repel head lice, for which it is also steeped in hot water and used to scrub the scalp. This seems to be a mostly European use for the plant, although it may have made its way into rural Appalachia or beyond.

YARROW
(achillea millefolium)

The yarrow plant has a long history of use as herbal medicine, and has also been implicated as useful in gardening (in the most literal sense) as well as rituals involving love and lust.

Yarrow has been hung in homes for centuries in order to ensure marital bliss- it has been hung above cradles to protect the recently born as well. It is sometimes worn by brides during a marriage, or worn by pregnant women to ensure easy and successful pregnancy.

It has been grown alongside grains and other plants to help prevent plant sickness- it attracts certain predatory insects which then attack pests, and may help prevent root diseases as well- literally the perfect guardian for any herbal or occult garden.

Yarrow stalks may be used as magical wands- they have also been used in i-ching, in which the divinatory rods used are normally made out of sections of yarrow stem. The plant is seen as able to predict the future. In some folk magick, people would literally shove a yarrow stem up their nose, with the idea that if the nose bled, their crush loved them, and if not, they needed to find another love interest. This is a fairly obvious bad idea.

It is thought that wearing a satchel containing yarrow to bed will allow a person to dream of their future loved one (whether it be a spouse, girlfriend, or whatnot.) Medicinally, yarrow is used by both Native tribes and other groups, to relieve headaches, common cold, and many other ailments- it is chewed as a mild stimulant, and may be applied to wounds to speed up healing.

When the stems or roots of the plant are steamed, the steam is considered a perfect cure for cough, or cold, which helps to break up a chest cold and does indeed act as an anti-inflammatory. For this reason, it can also be macerated and used on wounds to reduce pain and swelling.

When tea is made from the flowers of yarrow species, it can be drunk in order to cause the body to sweat out a fever. Some people may be allergic to yarrow and as such a medical professional should be consulted before it is used internally or topically. I have also heard of hemlock bark being used in a similar tea, to sweat out a fever; hemlock the pine tree, of course, not the extremely toxic herb ingested by Socrates, which ended his life. Yarrow is attractive and resembles, vaguely, a more colorful Queen Anne's Lace plant. The two are infrequently conflated and often grow in similar situations by road sides and in other disturbed areas.

CHAPTER SIX
Building and Maintaining an Occult Garden

For those who intend to grow their own herbs, or woody plants, to harvest them for occult purposes, creating the garden space itself can be a stumbling block, as some individuals are not well versed in the simple construction of garden beds, and in many cases, a person will attempt to design a small outdoor space to cultivate herbs only to be disheartened by failure.

The process itself however, is not difficult, and with a small amount of guidance and learning, anyone is capable of building and maintaining a small garden for occult purposes- this section will give suggestions for creating several types of garden beds, but using the same processes a person can expand their garden to larger sizes as need arises.

    The first step in building an occult garden is to simply determine the size which will be necessary, and to then take note of whether a large enough area can be set aside for its construction- for those who only intend to grow a very small number of plants, or who intend to use them for energetic protection rather than for harvesting, it is possible to simply install window boxes or grow the plants indoors (if they are able to be grown in potted form.)

    Climate is a major consideration- growing a tropical plant outdoors in a zone in which frost and snow last from November to April will require the plant to be uprooted and placed in a pot over winter- a process I myself have found tiring and unnecessary- it makes far more sense to grow plants that are suitable to the local climate, as even in most colder zones the majority the plants useful for occult purposes are able to be grown outdoors in a single season, or will act as biennials or perennials and will return to life after dying back for the winter.

Fruits of Eden, Herbalism and the Occult

To create and maintain a garden, the number of tools needed is actually far more limited than some believe- a hoe to break up soil, a shovel to dig the beds out, a small hand trowel for removing certain stubborn weeds, and, optionally, garden shears or a weed whacker to edge the borders (getting close enough to a lined bed with a lawn mower to cut down fringe weeds is difficult.) A rake can be employed to smooth and level the soil after it is tilled, although the soil does not need to be completely flat.

A garden plot does not need to be symmetrical or even- this is more of a concern if the garden is to be used to gather energy, or for feng shui, or for some decorative purpose- a strictly utilitarian plot used only to harvest herbs for potpourri, incense, or cuttings, needs only be properly tilled and cared for. My own garden is slightly irregular in the shaping and spacing of the beds, and this doesn't bother me even slightly.

In this section I have included some illustrations of several garden plots on my own property, in which I grow various plants. Even a garden of rather large size as mine is could be created in a single year with the proper tools, although I created mine over time.

My first suggestion is to border the garden- some individuals simply dig up the soil and plant on it, but for those who live in areas where the soil is not very rich, it makes sense to use a combination of compost, organic fertilizer, and (optionally) charcoal or bone to enrich it- this will make the topsoil far deeper, and thus a border is encouraged. This raises the soil level above the surrounding dirt outside of the garden, draining excess moisture, and helping to prevent some types of weeds from invading.

Borders for gardens range from stone harvested from the land itself (or a nearby river bed) to bricks, cement blocks, plastic siding, wooden planks, and in some areas, tree stumps or sod (clumps of grass that were lifted from the soil itself when it was first dug.)

Fruits of Eden, Herbalism and the Occult

Because the sod is likely to be chopped up and added to the compost pile, and because plastic siding usually warps over winter, stone or brick seem to be the best for siding a raised garden bed- I use brick in my own garden beds, but either will work- this has the additional benefit of allowing excess water to drain through gaps in the stone or brick, and brick especially tends to absorb the heat of the sun, which warms the soil a bit early in the spring allowing the soil to be tilled weeks before planting occurs. I have heard of people creating garden beds by taking half-bales of straw and simply dumping compost on top of them, growing plants on them; over time the straw degrades into soil, enriching these bale-beds even more. I have not tried it but it sounds simple.

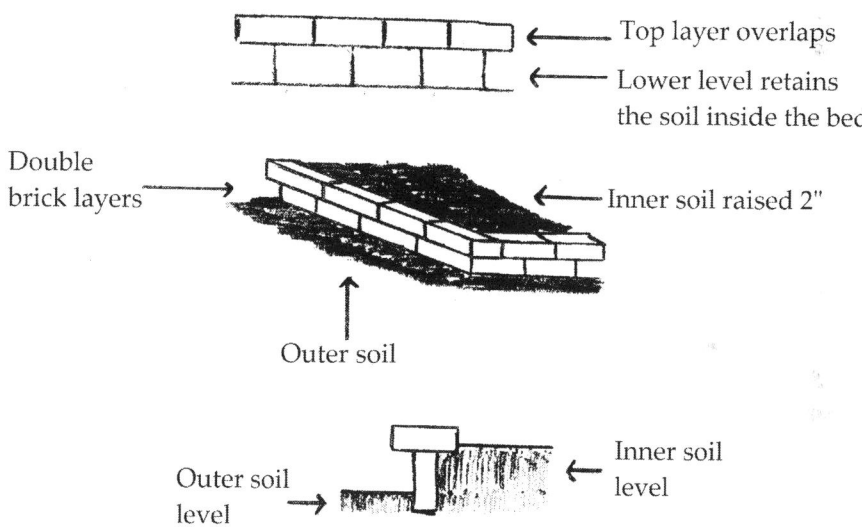

Brick will eventually degrade over time due to weathering- my own garden has been lined by the same bricks for almost a decade and they are more or less intact, but they will indeed decay into the soil, as water and cold chip away at its composition- this is hardly an issue most of the time, and brick allows a more even border to be created, whereas natural stone will produce an uneven (although attractive) border. If your property has many rocks in the soil these can be removed during tillage and placed around the tilled area, at no cost to the gardener. I was fortunate enough to get most of my bricks for free, from an abandoned local dam which was flooded out half a century ago.

    To create the raised bed, it is necessary to simply dig out the area to be turned into a bed, and subsequently a first level of brick is submerged halfway into the ground around the entire area- a second level of bricks is placed directly on top of the first (preferably with the bricks overlapping for added stability.) After winter these bricks will have shifted a bit, and some may have fallen out of the border, but it takes very little effort to correct this. Every second year, the bricks ought to be removed, and the border re-dug to remove certain types of grasses which will have endeavored to send shoots under the border, into the bed itself.

    Once the bed is raised several inches with the addition of compost, humus, bonemeal, charcoal, or other enriching materials, grasses and other weeds will have a much more difficult time attempting to invade the soil- this enriched, raised soil tends to be more productive, less prone to weed growth, and better drained, which helps to prevent diseases. I encourage all occult gardeners to build a compost pile- this prevents the degradation of soil and severely slows down erosion- for soil which is not enriched repeatedly eventually becomes less productive. (Composting also allows scraps from fruit and vegetables consumed from the garden or the store to become rich soil, which over time will build it up even more effectively than before with garden soil or humus alone.)

    To dig out the bed before bordering it, all that needs to be done is to remove the sod (grass and topsoil) with a shovel- break the roots apart with your hands and add the dirt back to the bed so that the topsoil is restored, and toss the grass into a compost pile- the resultant bed will already be tilled and loose and ready for planting as soon as the border and composting is complete.

For those who have not created a garden before, a small bed perhaps three feet wide by six feet long will suffice- this single, small bed will grow a multitude of herbs while requiring very little effort to maintain- I myself maintain a total of eight garden beds, two of which are substantially larger than this, for both occult and agricultural purposes, each lined and raised and enriched- only the largest bed is not composted, because it must contain soil loose enough for corn and beans in a companion planting method. Those who are already knowledgeable on creating and maintaining gardens can use whatever methods they have found to work.

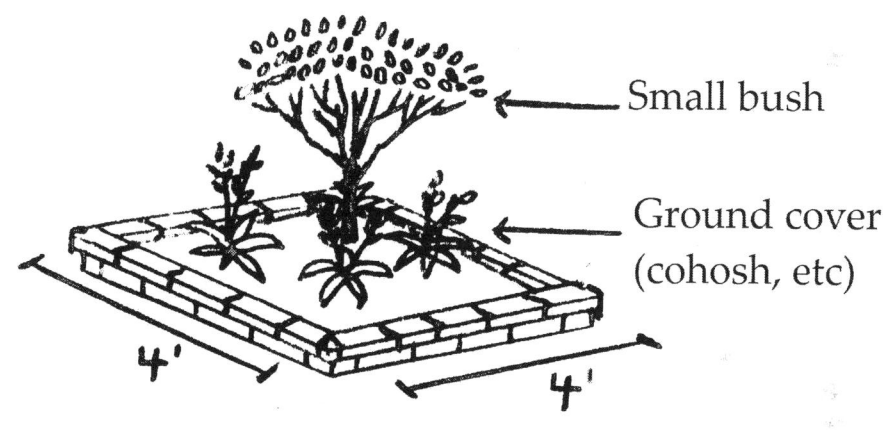

A small shade or half shade bed

Presumably, the garden you have now created is in an area that receives full sunlight- this is the best area for most plants which can be grown, but there are certain species that require some measure of shade in order to thrive- for these species, a garden bed may be constructed around the base of a deciduous tree (fruit trees- peach, apple, and so forth, are best,) perhaps three feet in radius, with the soil raised so as not to harm the roots of the tree when tilling the soil each year. Under no circumstances should beds be placed under pine trees- as the needles decay into a dry, inhospitable material which prevents most species from growing. (Those who wish to harvest amanitas should never disturb soil near pine or birch trees- which are the favorite hosts for this specific fungus.)

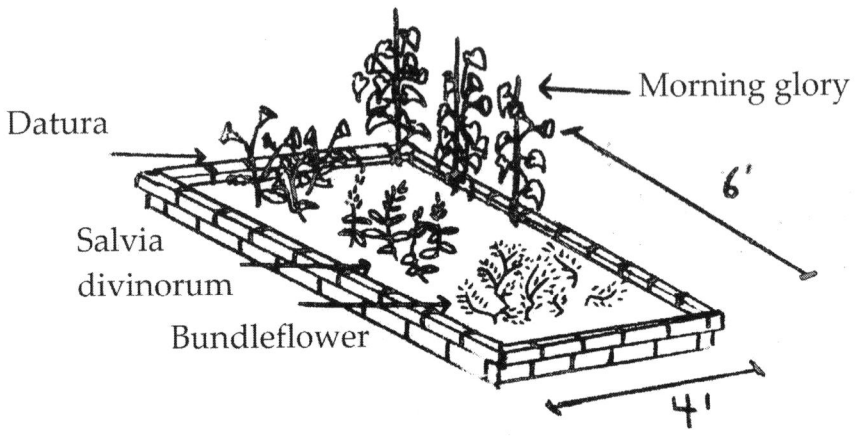

A small mind altering garden bed

Thankfully for the occult gardener, adding chemical fertilizer is usually not necessary if the soil has been properly enriched- a small amount of bonemeal mixed into the soil plus yearly composting will keep the soil rich, and the kinds of woody or herbaceous plants grown for spiritual purposes typically are not nutrient intensive, as they have not been artificially bred to grow larger, thus requiring intensive care to thrive. Herbs may require no fertilization at all to grow large and healthy- I added little to my herb bed other than some charcoal and poorly made compost and the plants there are just fine.

Once the garden has been dug, bordered, and enriched, it is essentially ready to plant- simply observing a zone map and your local climate will give you a clue of when to plant seeds (depending upon the type of plants desired.) Plants which have very low cold tolerance need to be planted slightly later than plants which tolerate some level of frost, which often need to be planted while weather is still cool- such plants, if put into the ground too late in the spring, will often not be able to germinate.

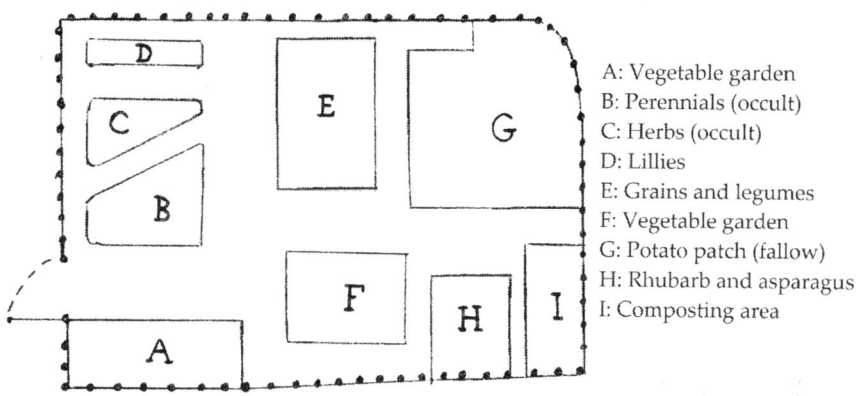

A: Vegetable garden
B: Perennials (occult)
C: Herbs (occult)
D: Lillies
E: Grains and legumes
F: Vegetable garden
G: Potato patch (fallow)
H: Rhubarb and asparagus
I: Composting area

A basic outline of my own garden setup. Overall dimensions are roughly 25' by 40'

Some of the plants listed here will grow best if the seeds are planted in the fall, before frost and snow comes (henbane and mullein notably so) so that the spring thaw can soak certain chemicals out of the seeds which delay germination- while they will still grow if planted in the early spring, some of the plants will, if this is attempted, either sprout and die, or not sprout at all.

A few of the plants listed in this book prefer a dry, warm climate (such as white sage) but it is still possible to grow them in a cooler, more wet climate if the bed has been raised, increasing temperature and draining excess moisture (another benefit of a raised, brick or stone lined garden bed.)

Because of the design of my own garden, I have not had much trouble with plant diseases except when they are, on a year to year basis, epidemic in the region- and because I have no specific knowledge of plant diseases beyond a few simple and common blights, I cannot give much in the way of advice on how to combat them- however, most occult plants have their own natural defenses against pests and germs, and will require no pesticides or other chemicals to grow properly. Here in Vermont, the most common disease of note only afflicts tomato plants.

There is another important point to make here: some of the plants listed (any of the mint plants, thistle, mullein, and a few others) spread aggressively, either through the release of extremely competitive seeds or using rhizomes or deep root systems which clone the plant each year- any plants listed in this book which are noted to spread aggressively should either have their own separate garden bed, or else be tightly controlled.

To control their spread, seed heads should be removed when dry, carefully, into a paper bag (never use plastic, as the seeds may rot- a paper bag helps regulate and remove excess moisture.) It is quite possible that some of the seeds will spread anyways- so if you see a plant out of place, and you do not wish for that species to spread, destroy the plant. Radishes will attempt to spread if allowed to go to seed- they and certain other species will seed in the fall, and you will clearly be able to see the seedlings coming up after the first frost- these can be dealt with through simply pulling them out.

There is also the matter of crop rotation to be considered, if the plants being grown tend to leech nutrients. Corn in particular rabidly eats up all available nitrogen, and indeed in many soils it won't even grow properly without added fertility (because man has bred them to grow large, thus requiring massive nutrient intake.) For any location where grains have been grown, to prevent leeching, erosion, and disease, the following year, some sort of legume should be planted in the area- mankind rotated crops in this manner for centuries before chemical fertilizers were in use, and in many cases did so even in the absence of knowledge of adding materials to the soil to enrich it. If you are going to plant the corn and beans together it is even more simplistic.

Thankfully, most herbs require fairly little nutrient content- perennials will spread over available areas for years without needing to be uprooted and separated or moved, and even annuals (especially those generally planted as flowers) don't particularly need special care unless they become diseased.

If disease is suspected in any of your crops, it is best to remove and burn diseased plant materials, and refrain from planting the same type of herb in that location for a year or two. It would take a fairly inordinate amount of explanation to note all of the common diseases and nutrient deficiencies which might cripple your plants- these things have already been explained in depth in other works, which can be found in the gardening or outdoors section of any good library (thus I do not need to list them here.) Many gardeners choose to test the pH of their soil (its acidity or alkalinity) with a professional service or a home kit before building their garden- or after doing so, with the goal of neutralizing their soil or very near so- I once added lime to my soil to prevent acidity, but most people in the world possess soil which is already within the tolerable range of most plants- swampy or very wet areas may have quite acidic soil and certain dry areas have a more alkaline soil.

A few of the plants listed in this work actually tend to enrich soil on their own (and in some areas are persistent and difficult to kill.) Clover, chamomile, and violets are chief among these species, and will thrive in most soils, resisting pests and deficiencies of most types- in fact if you're not in an arid climate and the clover fails to spread, something is probably very wrong with the soil.

As for the growth of some of the marsh-dwelling plants listed, they may indeed already be growing wild in some areas, but they are possible to cultivate especially if your property is near a marsh or other source of fluid- it is of course possible to build artificial terrain, flooding an area to create a pond or paddies, but this is extremely intensive and would cost a great deal- the average occultist can safely stick with growing a few raised beds to supply most of their herbal needs.

There are also plants with an intrinsic spiritual value which may be grown in any occult garden to great effect- a search online will turn up scores of plants which enrich the air quality (such as boston ferns, which have no real occult value of their own) while pennyroyal and the ever-loved chamomile purify the soil- for those in the mystic practice who value purity and would like to drive negative forces away from their space, these plants are invaluable. The number of Roman Chamomile plants in my garden has increased from roughly two plants in 2012, which sprouted from seeds I planted, to five plants in 2013, a dozen in 2014, and now roughly thirty which have cropped up, randomly scattered among the beds this current year, which will surely be joined by others come the next spring. A bumper crop of free tea, indeed.

I will herein describe my own setup- for while my garden is quite large, the area dedicated solely to the occult is quite small (for no more space is needed for my own purposes) indeed, even the creation of this one bed seems a fortunate mystic experience- for the peach tree acting as its aesthetic centerpiece (which allows me to grow shade-loving species in the bed) grew on its own, apparently from a stray peach pit that germinated from the composting process.

The base of the tree itself being surrounded by purely decorative hostas, the remainder of the bed is populated by wild-growing violets, in and around which a mixture of basil, chamomile, catnip, and various other herbs were sown, all of which grew rapidly in the half-shady area- a few decorative perennials on the other side ensure that these delicate plants are shaded from sunlight coming from the south, which would have withered them.

I have also false dittany growing in the bed- but this particular plant either dislikes the location or is spending a great deal of its time growing a root system, because it remains a rather small plant compared to how *dictamnus alba* normally flushes out into a small shrubby perennial- however, it is still alive, so it may be planning to bloom at some future date. It, too, has grown larger above the soil, but the roots must be massive by now.

I am a fan of aesthetic gardening- for my own occult purposes it was important to create a rich, lush, beautiful outdoor ritual space, the center of which is open to allow movement during rituals- the beds, thus, are gathered largely around this central space, with the beds further away from this area reserved mostly for growing edible species- some of those edible species (corn and radishes notably) are also used in some occult workings.

The presence of various life forms in the garden greatly increases its usefulness for positive rituals, and rituals designed to draw off of the energies of nature- the presence of stones, specially chosen for their own energies also enhances this nature- although it is also possible to use a reverse method to create a sort of desecrated ritual space designed to enhance negative energies to perform darker rites- in theory, this could consist of choosing an already negative location and further damaging it, perhaps through salting the area, erecting tombstone-style monuments to darkness, and generally filling the region with dark spells, sowing various poisonous or thorn-ridden species that will repel most life forms from entering the area. Indeed, nature itself creates such dreary spaces seemingly with the goal of providing a flip-side to the bright, butterfly-filled meadow- and herein is a short revelation about the nature of nature itself:

Writ short, nature being a whole rather than a half, both those who look upon it as an evil force, and those who look upon it with optimistic positivity, are wrong. Nature is both creator and destroyer, and for every breadbasket filled with the fruits of the ground, is a tomb in which there lies one dead from disease or starvation. These dreary, seemingly accursed locations are the result of the inability of the natural state of existence to be completely stable- much like upon the sun there are spots of low and high activity, the planet itself is a changing form, with phases, cycles, and partitions, where there appear zones of high and low energy, zones of positive and negative forces. I have seen no better example of this than comparing two locations in my own region- one, a sort of grove deep in the forest which remains green even during winter, and where a gentle sort of natural spring conjoins a small river (a field of extremely positive energy, to say so in a non-new age, non-crystal worshiping manner) and another location not far from it, where the trees are all dead, the area is bereft of all sounds of animal life, and in which, occasionally, can be felt a sort of hot wind which comes from nowhere. The Gnostics may have said it best in their own philosophical murmurings when they remarked upon the nature of the corrupted sphere of existence being arranged into opposition- that is, the constructed dichotomies understood and observed by man. Good and evil, up and down, and so forth.

In the first location, despite the constant noise of life happily progressing, there is a sense of serenity- and this location I have used for rituals which include a healing, positive element. In the second location, where life stands still (and which might be best termed a black hole of negative energy) the lack of life and presence of blasts of hot wind seem to indicate an accursed proclivity- indeed, the air coming out of that location is so warm that I have to compare it to the hot winds of Texas- despite the fact that the area was, at the time I first found it, frosted, barren, and the soil frozen solid in opposition to the hot air above.

Even within a single property, energy may vary- use this to your benefit during rituals, and even during the conceptual design of your own occult garden bed or beds. You may have one spot near your home that is lush, vibrant, and green, where you plant the "nice" or "happy" species, and a darker, more forsaken spot where you place the stinging nettles and yew tree.

CHAPTER SEVEN
Making Charcoal and its Uses

Charcoal is immensely important- although its use is entirely optional; it has three major purposes, firstly, for the making of incense, secondly, as a soil additive for making terra preta or similar mixes, and thirdly, for use as a cleaner fuel for rituals (for hardwood lump charcoal, made in your own backyard, is unmatched.)

  A forewarning to all readers; it is prudent to check with your local fire marshal before attempting to make charcoal- the process relies on open flame, which may be banned (or seasonally so) in your area, usually depending on rainfall. Never attempt to create charcoal during a drought, or without a source of water nearby (preferably, a hose which can be used to extinguish any spreading flame.) Some towns, counties, states, and nations, have rather arcane ordinances and laws regarding burning material, and while carbonizing woody flesh to make charcoal is not an uncontained or open burn, per se, it is usually regulated as though it was.

  If you do not live in an area where charcoal can be made, it can normally be bought in large bags as hardwood lump (do not bother to buy briquettes, especially those infused with flammable fluids- they are useless.) This is fairly inexpensive, but for those who intend to use it as a soil additive to a great degree, larger quantities need to be made, and there are several fairly easy methods to do so, listed and described here.

  The use of charcoal dates back many centuries- most often it seems to have been used as a fuel which was more readily used and cleaner burning than wood alone. Originally, it was created in enormous pits, where wood was laid and set ablaze, allowed to begin smoldering to ash before being buried, creating an anaerobic burn which carbonized the wood without turning it to ash- these pits would burn for weeks and supply extremely large quantities of material, but were abandoned in favor of kilns, and recently, backyard charcoal-making has expanded as its use in soil enrichment and as a carbon negative fuel has been rediscovered. At other times it has been made in small drums for use in art, and has also been made by stacking wood under a layer of dirt; this practice being the job, in Medieval times, of the *collier*.

For my own purposes, I normally create charcoal and add it to my soil rather than try and make it into incense or for anything else. This methodology, called *terra preta,* reverses soil erosion by restoring carbon. Most soils, especially those which have been used for agriculture for long periods, tend to have very little carbon left, as it is slowly leeched by plants and ingested in food crops or burned as fuel from wood. A typical suburban lawn is also carbon poor; it has been cleared and not allowed to lie undisturbed for some time, reducing aggregates and relying on chemical fertilizer. Often, it is also tainted by the use of herbicides, and by other pollutants.

The process of enriching soil in this manner seems to have coincided with Amazonian culture quite some time ago- indeed, the soil itself is actually being mined on a small scale and sold as potting mix or is spread across Brazilian agricultural fields, which increases yield dramatically. The discovery of yards-deep and miles-wide stretches of charcoal enriched soil actually revealed that a culture was able to create an agricultural space for itself in the notoriously thin and nutrient poor Amazonian soils. (It has been suggested that the natives managed to blanket an area the size of Britain in terra preta, in some cases 10 feet deep.) Until the discovery of this soil's benefits, it was considered impossible for a substantial and partially urbanized culture to exist there; a conundrum since the region also contains numerous megaliths- hundreds of stone pyramids, among other remains. Only the now famous terra preta was able to explain how they were able to produce enough food for a stable culture.

Terra preta has several major benefits related to agriculture.

Fruits of Eden, Herbalism and the Occult

The first benefit is the composition of the soil. With richer carbon inclusion and with the structure of charcoal being as it is, the soil aggregates present in any good agricultural tilth are much increased.

The second benefit is yield. Terra preta, properly created, or even soil merely modest in composition to which carbon is added, tends to produce larger, faster growing crops. I have tested this myself in a semi-scientific manner and it does indeed work; and drastically so. It appears to be most useful when the species grown are fruiting (tomato plants, squash, etc) and least effective for grains, possibly because grains are used to thinner soils. No two charcoal infused beds are likely to be exactly the same in composition but academia has vouched for its efficacy as well, so on that token I presume my results have been replicated under better, more controlled conditions.

The third benefit is related to survival of the plants grown. Terra preta encourages worms to move in and discourages various pests. Slugs and snails appear to dislike the carbon dust that is present; perhaps it causes them to dry out. It also apparently bothers moles, which are present and common in and around my property, but seem to dig *around* beds infused with charcoal but not through them.

The fourth benefit is related to precipitation. A terra preta soil resists both inundation (which can rot plants, especially root crops) and drought (which is deadly to most species.) The porous molecules present store water away from the roots when it is quite wet, and release it when it is more dry- a sort of time release of moisture.

Normally, about 10 to 20 percent charcoal is added to the soil, to a depth which may range from six inches to several feet. It is further amended with compost and, in some cases, bonemeal. I have heard of some individuals also including shards of terra cotta (clay) or pea stones. I am not sure this is, strictly speaking, necessary or has any additional effect upon yield, survival, or anything else. The clay sherds added appear to be an attempt to exactly replicate the authentic Amazonian terra preta; but in this case the sherds are probably just archaeological remains deposited over time, accidentally or coincidentally, rather than purposefully and pragmatically.

Increasingly, businesses are springing up to create charcoal for agricultural purposes- as a way of restoring soil destroyed by decades of mechanized farming- these charcoals are referred to as "biochar" and seem to be finding a niche market among farmers who have more long term goals in mind, as traditional amendment methods using treated sewage or composted materials typically only restore the soil for a few years before they have in turn been degraded, while an addition of charcoal mixed with more traditional amendment materials can last for many decades before it degrades, if the soil being worked is being worked mechanically, as is the case on most farms, that is. If it is being worked manually, for example by a hobby gardener with a rake, shovel, and hoe, it will last longer than they will- the Amazonian soils are many centuries old and were probably farmed for the entire life span of whatever strange culture existed there and used it.

METHOD 1: THE SIMPLE BARREL

To create charcoal, one of several arrangements is necessary- either with a simple barrel method, a retort, or else a sort miniature pit method which I have not tested myself but which is said to be effective for small batches. It is also possible to use the ages-old pit method to create enormous quantities of charcoal, but it is so intensive (and usually not necessary) to create that amount, that unless you intend to spread it across several acres and make a survivalist sort of miniature farm, this method is best left alone.

To utilize the simple drum method (which, for my own small scale creation of charcoal is fine) you are simply erecting a 55 gallon steel oil drum on your land. This drum will have a series of small holes drilled in the bottom. Raise the drum an inch or so above the surrounding soil by mounding a ring of dirt around up under its outer edge. Leave a two or three inch slot for air to enter under the barrel. The holes can be small or large- it seems to make little difference. My own barrel has numerous 1/8 inch holes, but the best method I have seen utilizes seven half inch holes- one in the very center of the barrel, and six arranged in a hexagon around it, roughly four inches from the center. This allows air to be drawn in by the rising, hot gas resulting from the burn, meaning air is not coming in at the top of the barrel- this results in a mostly anaerobic and continuous burn.

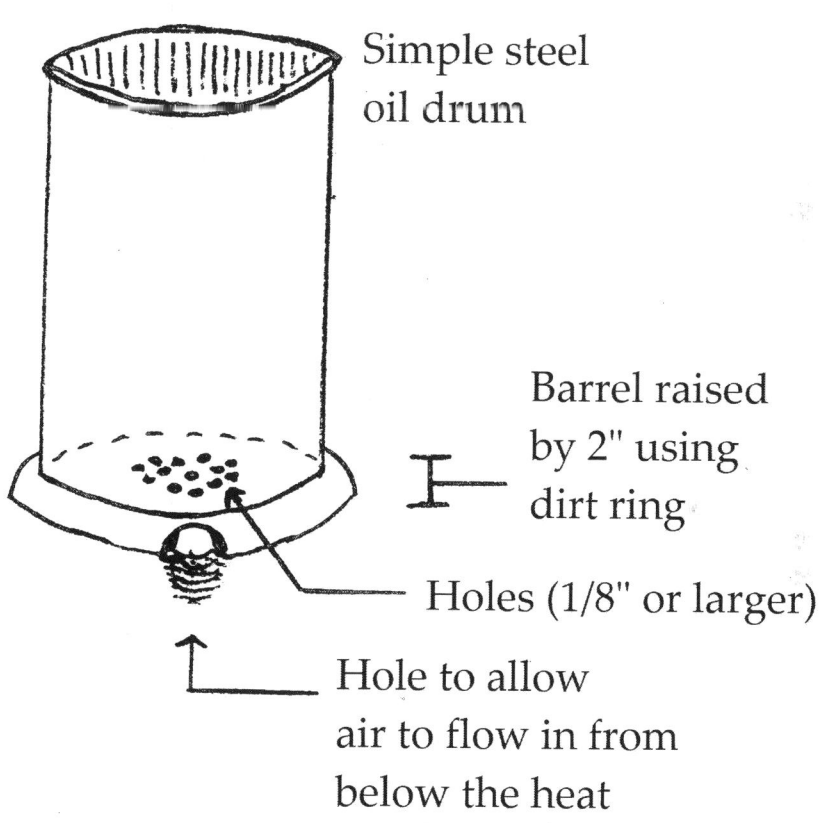

Fruits of Eden, Herbalism and the Occult

In the bottom of the barrel, some sort of kindling will be needed as the fire must become extremely hot- for those insisting on purely organic substances this can be dry leaves and small branches, plus straw or any other easily ignited debris- but newspapers, partially crumpled into balls, will work wonders- upon these, branches are piled. This is a fairly decent way to dispose of newspapers, cardboard waste, and so forth, immolating them to perform the burn, cutting down on the amount that goes to a landfill (except where such things are recycled.)

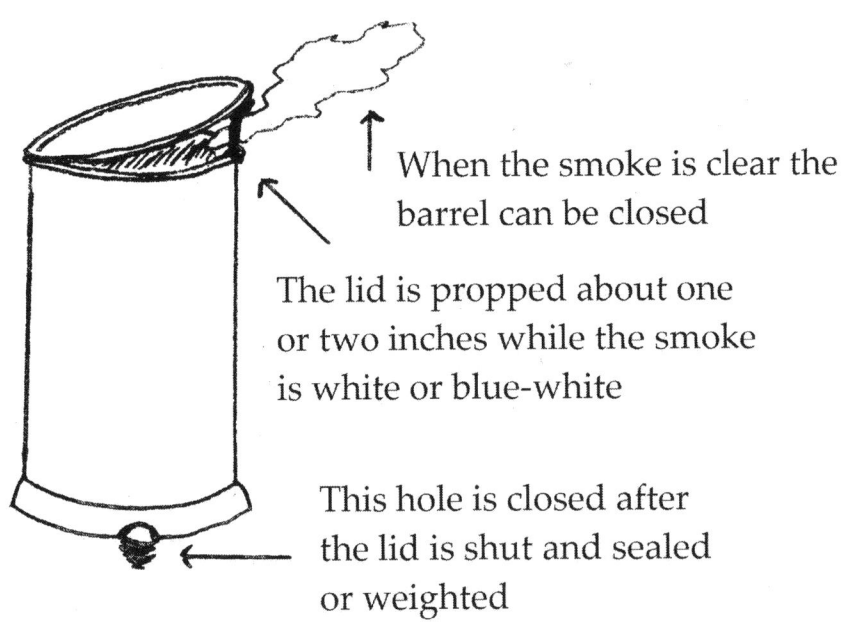

When the smoke is clear the barrel can be closed

The lid is propped about one or two inches while the smoke is white or blue-white

This hole is closed after the lid is shut and sealed or weighted

It is important to build the kindling in a ring around the outside edge of the barrel- if your kindling is blocking the holes in the barrel it will not be effective. The yield of charcoal will be far higher if you leave a space several inches wide from the bottom of the barrel to the very top of whatever material is to be added- this acts like a chimney and creates suction, drawing air from below to sustain the burn. Often, wedges are placed at the bottom of the barrel to lift the burning material a few inches to spread the inflowing air around.

The material which is to become carbonized (that is, charcoal) should be lengths of wood small enough to fit into the barrel allowing the lid to be closed- if the lid has a rubber sealant around the rim it needs to be removed, as it will melt together if you fail to do so. Once the kindling has caught and the small kindling branches begin to burn, begin tossing these segments in around the sides, careful to arrange it so that the central area is mostly devoid of material- you should be able to see the holes in the bottom of the barrel despite filling it with wood.

A word to the wise; hardwood creates a far better charcoal than pine or similar woods: pine tends to form almost metallic-looking lumps which flake apart but are more difficult to grind, whereas hardwoods create a loose, easily crushed charcoal which you will be able to make quick work of. Corn cobs, sunflower or corn stalks, and some other materials, can also be carbonized, yielding as much charcoal as their content of woody material.

The lengths of wood (which should be split into smaller pieces from their progenitor limbs) should be between one and two inches in diameter- any smaller branches used for kindling will also provide small lumps which can be ground up for use as well. I have carbonized piles of very small twigs and branches and the yield, while lower, is still large enough to grind and add to the garden soil. In this manner most of the garden is now carbonized heavily.

Make sure to wear gloves for this work. Have something handy to prop the lid open slightly while it cooks. The final step is this- once you are done stacking the branches or segments of wood around the outside of the barrel, close the lid but leave a gap of about an inch or two, propping it open with a rock, brick, branch, or something of that nature. The material inside will be getting air from below, sustaining a smolder without open flame- a mostly anaerobic burn that ensures you get more charcoal than ash (although ash can just be ground in with the charcoal, adding phosphate.)

The amount of time required is variable. Usually the key is that white smoke means it is not ready yet, and no smoke means all organic material has been burned and the charcoal has begun to break down into ash. Thus, it is best to check the barrel's contents when the smoke becomes a bluish color. Simply use a branch to lift the lid and peer inside. If the branches appear brown, let it keep cooking a bit longer. If they are black you can close it up. If they are black and some white flakes are appearing on them, it's definitely time to close it. The wood will have shrunk in size as everything except the carbon is burned off- this is normal. A full barrel will yield at most half a barrel of charcoal unless the method is extremely efficient.

Leave the barrel alone overnight- otherwise cinders may spark up- grinding charcoal is dangerous if live embers are present, as charcoal powder is extremely flammable. I have found it easier and more dust-free to add a half gallon or so of water to the charcoal before grinding, and it makes it safer to do so as well.

You will be left with a small amount of ash in the bottom of the barrel, with many small chunks of charcoal which used to be kindling, and branches and limbs which will have mostly carbonized- put on a pair of gloves and grab each length, placing it into a plastic barrel, and run your hands up and down, to dislodge carbonized material into the barrel for grinding, and place any still-brown materials back into the steel drum for the next burn. If the burn was efficient you can just pile everything in the plastic barrel. Do not fill it more than halfway or the grinding takes longer. It is possible to grind the charcoal within the steel drum, but lifting it into a wheelbarrow to sift it will be difficult for some, and the danger of a spark causing the charcoal to ignite is higher if you do not water the contents first.

After many burns the barrel will be full of small chunks of charcoal which will be mixed with the present ash- ash itself has its own nutrient value as well, so the small amount which will end up ground up with the charcoal is negligible in harm. Ash can also be

Fruits of Eden, Herbalism and the Occult

added to compost piles to enrich them.

You must use wood to grind the charcoal- *do not use anything metallic under any circumstances*. Metal may create sparks, and a spark plus finely powdered charcoal means "small, hot explosion able to sear off your hair and cause first degree burns." Some occultists may not care if they have eyebrows and hair on their forearms but others may desire to keep them.

The grinding will yield roughly one part fine powder and one part small chunks and grains. Anything you grind should be strained into a wheelbarrow or other container through a medium mesh screen- fine mesh removes the small chunks which themselves are good.

A more efficient, anoxic setup such as a kiln or fully modified retort will be far better for producing charcoal for any chemical purpose; for gardening it does not matter if the charcoal contains some resins and ash (because both add nutrients to the soil itself- ash and its phosphates are important for root crops especially) but if the intent is to use it for incense or other purposes, it has to be as pure as possible- you will want only carbon, at least to a degree that is possible without an industrial setup. The theoretical possibility of making a brick and cement kiln for a completely anoxic burn exists, but the setup required is probably beyond the engineering skills of most of the population (I have thought of making such a kiln myself because I require a great deal of charcoal for my own large garden setup but so far have stuck with merely the modified barrel and would probably just add a second barrel instead, given the choice to do so.)

Illustrations are here provided.

METHOD 2: THE RETORT

The retort is coming into much more wide use as the most efficient method of making charcoal which can be done without obtaining a high grade kiln- the retort is somewhat similar to a simple barrel burn, and is made by taking the same oil drum and turning it on its side and modifying it slightly.

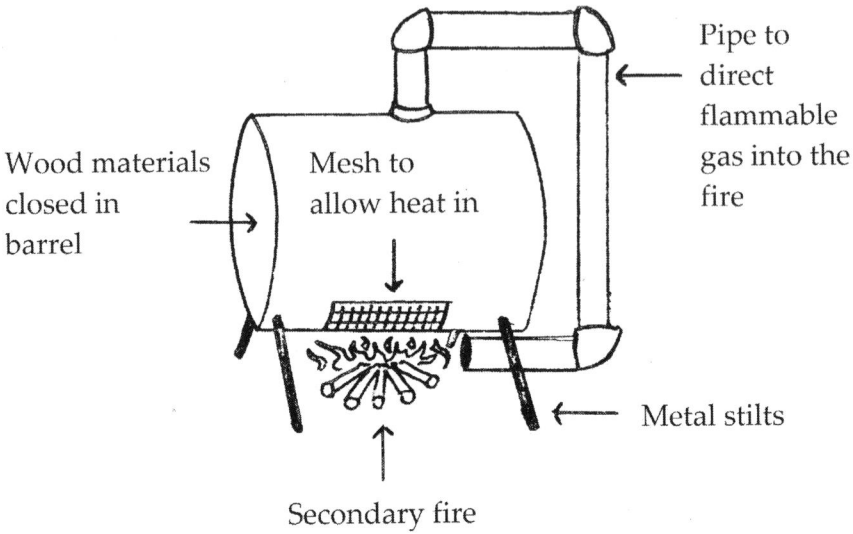

The basic design is a set of short legs which elevate the barrel, the bottom side of which has a series of small holes or vents cut into it, with a hole punched also into the top of the barrel, around which is welded a pipe system, that is meant to vent volatile oils released by burning wood back into the fire, which is kindled below the retort- this intensifies the flame, and heats the unit nicely, creating a higher quality charcoal. The reader who wishes to construct a retort may find basic designs and plans on the internet in addition to the basic illustration here.

Additionally, because the flame itself is separate from the contents of the drum, the entire drum can be filled with split lengths of limb which will carbonize more efficiently than with the simple drum-on-the-ground method. This process is also supposedly carbon-negative, for those whose views of the world require a more environmentalist slant. My theory is that the simple barrel is also carbon negative considering the amount of carbon created.

While a retort is infinitely more efficient and easy to use, it does require some basic knowledge to construct- I myself have held off from doing so primarily because I do not possess the tools needed to properly machine a retort- as steel drums are quite durable and a regular drill has a difficult time cutting through the sides. Even cutting the holes in the drum as I have takes some effort, at first making small holes and then enlarging them using a power drill.

However, those who do possess basic engineering skills should consider a retort before merely burning limbs in a barrel- it takes me two burns to attain the same amount of charcoal (and at a slightly lower quality) as would be yielded by a single burn in a 55 gallon drum retort- a retort is probably also somewhat safer, being more properly contained.

The basic concept however is the same- the burning itself is separate from most of the woody material being cooked. It's the same idea as a kiln where the carbonizing material is separated from the burn chamber entirely. There's an interesting bit of history to be stated regarding the design of the infamous brazen bull- the metal bull which was used to burn its own designer alive. The chamber was anaerobic and the skeleton of the condemned was cooked much like charcoal, such that the bone reportedly became metallic and shone like jewelry, for which it was then extracted and used. Of course, I do not endorse or condone cooking prisoners in a drum retort.

METHOD 3: THE CAMPFIRE

In what must be the most simplistic method of all, charcoal can be created (albeit in small amounts) by merely constructing a campfire, letting it get red hot, dousing it with water, and letting it smolder with some dirt piled around it to exclude oxygen. When wood is burned, it takes some time for the carbon itself to be cooked off after all other materials have already been exhausted. This is useful only for getting a small amount of charcoal, and is low efficiency. Those with the inability to machine a few holes in a steel drum can use this method but it's less environmentally friendly and really yields enough only for potted houseplants or maybe window boxes. Very small charcoal batches, usually for artistic use, can also be made by putting twigs in a steel can, then inverting it over a small fire.

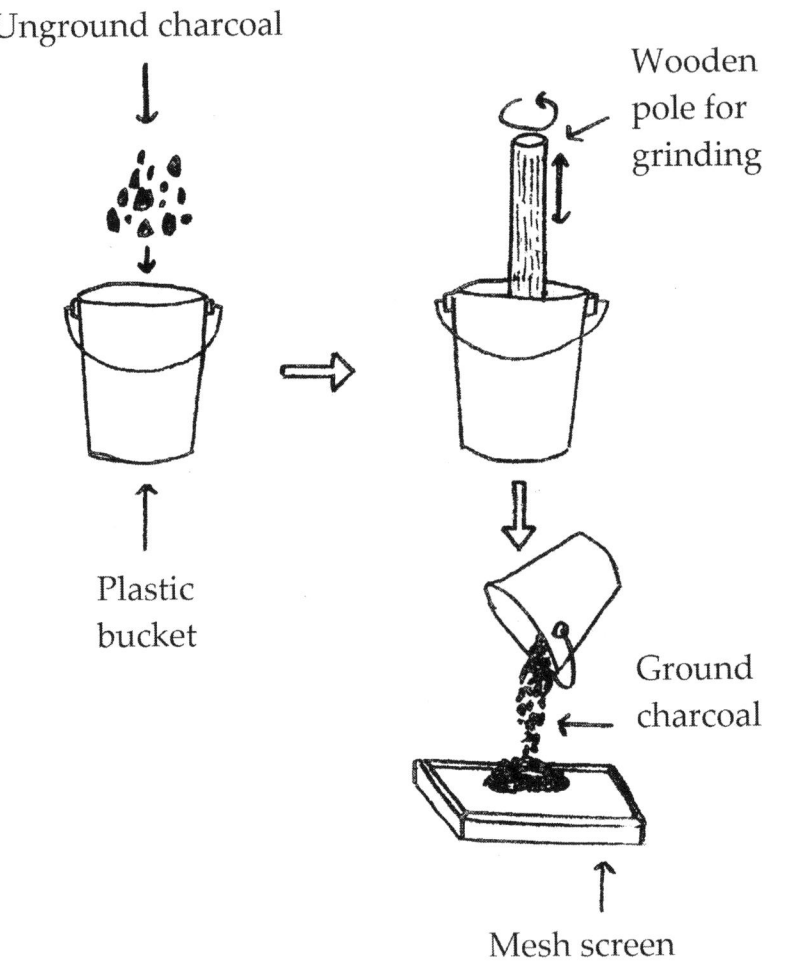

Fruits of Eden, Herbalism and the Occult

THE IMPORTANCE OF CHARCOAL IN THE OCCULT AND ITS USE

Charcoal is one of the more important substances within the mystic world- not only is it a source of fuel for rituals which might involve fire (and for which a great deal of smoke from, say, a wood fire, is not desired) and the basis for the creation of incense, but as a soil additive is unmatched.

To the ancient alchemists experimenting with fireworks, medicine, and other processes and creations, charcoal was equally useful, forming the basis of various antidote compounds and also that of gunpowder. Even today, charcoal "smoothies" are used to purge those overdosing on drugs or alcohol in a clinical setting.

It is also useful in the creation of sigils, as it is a staple in the artistic world, creating a smudgy, black outline when used as a stylus upon paper (which is preferably of a rough quality.) This forms a naturalistic and qualitative improvement over, say, using a black marker on printer paper, and is just as cheap if you're making your own charcoal- possibly cheaper. While making the charcoal I suppose the occultist might want to experiment with pyromancy, but that is entirely optional. Cooking charcoal is also fairly amusing, for those who are interested in fire- although the flame itself dies when the lid is propped. On a cold autumn day, standing by the charcoal barrel is fairly comforting, especially if the wood being cooked off is fragrant; hickory, maple, and peach wood are all good for this purpose, as is any pine.

It is also a useful way for those with wooded land to efficiently clear brush without wasting the wood. Bonfire burns are fun but this reduces the wood to ash- which is great for planting potato plants and useless for restoring soil on a permanent basis. Any small chunks of charcoal in the soil will still be there long after you're nothing more than a grinning skeleton or perhaps a pile of ashes yourself.

    My own property contains a relatively small wooded area- perhaps a quarter acre in size or smaller, and in this one single year I have already created six batches of charcoal almost entirely using just branches and chunks of log and twig from this area. It is also now cleaned out and looks better than it previously did. If you possess a larger area of forest you may consider applying unprocessed charcoal right back into the forest soil to eventually turn it black. Just as a forest is greenest after a forest fire (because of the charcoal and ash added to the soil) so too will the trees be potentially greener for such a thing.

CHAPTER EIGHT
Making incense, ink, paper, and smudges naturally

This chapter is intended as a basic guide to the creation of various ritual goods using natural substances- some of which are of great importance and can be made in small batches as the occultist requires- skills that are necessary for a truly isolated occult practice- the market for such things is crowded with consumers and short on creators of good quality, and as such these goods can be expensive, but are far more easy to create than some surmise.

CREATING NATURAL INCENSE

Tools needed:

- Mortar and pestle (preferably granite or other hard stone)
- Herbs, resins, woods, or other goods, either ground up beforehand to powder or to be ground in the mortar
- Finely powdered charcoal
- Makko powder, enough to add 25% by weight to your incense mix
- Distilled water
- A flat surface large enough for your prepared incense mix
- A very large number of bamboo or similar incense sticks, of your preferred length

Any incense uses charcoal as a base- if you have already created (or intend to create) your own charcoal, you are now well ahead in planning to create your own incense- the other materials for its creation will vary depending upon the style of incense created, as it can be formed into coils, cones, sticks, or merely remain granulated, placed upon a lit charcoal tab and allowed to smoke.

The most commonly used form of charcoal incense in the

western world is the simple stick. Normally, it is composed of a mix of powdered charcoal, makko powder (which you can find for sale online for low prices- it's unlikely you will have the means to create your own makko) and some sort of herbal scent, which can be raw, powdered herbs, extracted compounds, or powdered resins- if you have constructed your own occult garden, and dried some of your herbs (don't use any which are narcotic or toxic when burned) you may choose to grind them for use.

You will need, additionally, some implement for the grinding process- a stone mortar and pestle works well (and will not break easily) although other implements exist. Resist the temptation to invest in a cheaper ceramic mortar and pestle, as these are not capable of being used to grind some of the tougher substances you may desire, and because of the smoothness of the vessel, the process is more difficult. I accidentally destroyed my own ceramic mortar years ago attempting to grind relatively soft substances.

Any materials you grind will probably need to be sifted as well- a flour sifter might already be in your kitchen (make sure to wash it afterwards.) This will remove larger granules of material which will screw up the burning process. For any substance which is hard to grind, such as wood, roots, etc, it may be better to simply purchase the raw material in ground up form at a store.

Whatever loose, ground up mix you have created, regardless of its content, ought to sit, enclosed, overnight, allowing the scents to blend (although this is by no means necessary, and is purely recommended.)

The rest of the process, up until the rolling, is very simple- weigh your ground up herbs, woods, resins, or whatever you have decided to add to the incense, and add roughly 25% makko powder by weight (to act as a binder, making the sticks durable) into your bowl and, optionally (but recommended to increase its combustibility) 10% of its weight in charcoal powder. Add distilled water slowly, kneading the mixture until it has a loose, almost putty-like quality (you may accidentally add too much water on your first try, destroying the mix- oh well.)

For your final step, you will need to take this large lump of material and slap it onto a board or other flat surface- it will be far easier to roll your sticks on a flat surface than trying to pull the material in strands out of your bowl.

Take a strand of the putty-ish incense "dough" and place it an inch or two above the bottom of one of your bamboo sticks- roll the stick slightly back and forth with one hand, and spread the material over the stick in a direction opposite the empty length of stick, until it is fully coated with incense- spread it fairly thin, and try to make it even, but don't go insane if your first few sticks fail (for a visual representation of how this process is achieved, you can use the internet and pull up a large number of "making incense" or "rolling incense sticks" related videos.)

Cut or pinch off the strand just slightly above the end of the bamboo stick- this stick is now complete and should be hung by its empty end or otherwise positioned so that it can dry without the soft, doughy coating contacting any object- in this manner it will dry over time. You can also fill jars with your incense sticks, making sure to vent them a few times every day to release ambient moisture.

If the resulting mix does not burn well, try adding a small amount more makko and/or charcoal to the mix the next time around- if it has a weak scent, add more of your other ingredients. It may take a bit of trial and error, but once you have mastered this technique, you can enjoy incense at perhaps a tenth the cost of buying it.

To make incense cones, simply mix the dough as before, but pinch off small pieces (about the size of a cherry) of the doughy mix and form them with your hands into cones (which are unlikely to be aesthetically attractive- but will burn nonetheless.) These cones, formed, should be flattened on the bottom, so that they are able to be stood up to burn. You can place them on wax paper, flat end on the bottom, to dry.

It is also possible to form the incense dough into small, round, pea sized pellets (which is even easier as shape doesn't matter- deformed pellets are fine) and simply burned on a hot plate or directly/indirectly on a charcoal tablet. While using tablets or other methods to smolder granular incense made as such is slightly more expensive than self-sustaining cones or sticks, it is still cheaper than buying it.

Almost any combination of scented herbs, resins, woods, etc, can be combined into an incense mix- but, using the index at the end of this book, you can choose two or three ingredients for mixes which have similar natures (IE, healing, attracting love, protecting the home, curses.) You can also stick with a single ingredient rather than creating a mix- lavender is particularly good for this due to its pleasing aroma and strong scent.

The process of creating incense can be somewhat time consuming, but even a single small batch, once properly mastered, should last an extremely long period of time- batches may in some cases be created which can supply the home with daily scent for months or even years at a time. A few hundred incense sticks is typical, but it is possible for a single person, well trained in these practices, to create many thousands in a single day.

Again, it is important to remember that charcoal, in particular, is not a necessary ingredient- it is solely added to stabilize the incense and make it easier to ensure that it burns properly- incense can be made just with makko, but mastering the percentage to use by weight varies depending upon the ingredients used, whereas charcoal is added at the same or a similar rate despite recipe changes.

In the east, incense is often processed into coils- however this process would be extremely time consuming to do by hand, and is most often done with machines in this era- the only major benefits of these dense, thick coils, is that the incense lasts much longer when being transported, maintaining its fragrance, and that it has an exceptionally long burn time (sometimes several days.) Its aroma is also stronger because of the thickness of the applied charcoal mixes- but coils are uncommon in the western world due to the relatively inexpensive nature of cones and sticks, and their ease of creation.

    There is also a Japanese method of creating incense which is its own stick (that is, it is not kneaded around a bamboo or other wooden core)- these sticks are usually shorter and prone to breaking and chipping easily, so the quality is somewhat lower- it would also require a mold to be created which could take some time.

    For those who wish to craft their own mold for making cones (or sticks) it can be done by those with some skill in carving soapstone- this can be used to craft sticks and cones which are almost uniform in size and quality, with relatively little effort- the use of a Dremel or similar device can simplify the process.

    Simply take a block of soapstone which is flat on the bottom, and cut it using a saw, roughly in half lengthwise- you will then need to carve out the area to be filled on both the bottom and top halves- I have worked with soapstone before, although I have not used it to make molds but rather statuettes or totems. Soapstone is available online or in some stores (usually those with a gardening center, or else stores focusing on arts and crafts) for extremely low prices for relatively large blocks- it will likely take multiple attempts to create a working mold, but once created it can be used to very quickly make a large number of cones or sticks. A single two-sided stone can be filled with multiple such molds, if they are being used for these relatively small works, especially Japanese style core-free sticks.

Fruits of Eden, Herbalism and the Occult

CREATING YOUR OWN INK FROM NATURAL INGREDIENTS

Multiple plants are useful in the creation of inks which can be made in enormous quantities- these ink recipes listed here are only particularly useful for those who intend to use a dipping pen (trying to fill a ballpoint pen with these inks may result in their destruction) or for those who intend to use calligraphy in order to decorate their literary works (a book of shadows, or something of that nature), or for the creation of beautiful, highly stylized sigils for the evocation process. The three given processes produce rich brown, a dark blue, and deep red inks respectively, and upon drying they will dull slightly- illuminating your manuscripts with these ink will yield far better results than the chemically processed inks generally used in the modern age- it also saves an enormous amount of money, as the price of the ingredients is far lower than the price of the number of pens which they replace.

MAKING BLACK WALNUT INK

Making ink from black walnut husks is quite easy- you may choose to grow your own trees (although it will be some years before they are ready to harvest from) or, if you are in the right climate, you may simply get some from a neighbor- they are also often found on the internet, but you *must* obtain black walnuts which still have the outer husk, which is not the same as the hard inner shell. These husks, and not the nuts inside, are the useful part of the plant for making ink- recipes for this ink are available online but this is the easiest method I have found. The nuts themselves, once de-husked, are edible.

Rest assured that any object or surface touched by the husk will be marked with a dark brown stain, even before the materials are processed. As such, it makes sense to wear gloves and not to plan to use many of the implements used for creating this ink for any other purpose, at least until they have been voraciously scrubbed.

Fruits of Eden, Herbalism and the Occult

Peel the husks off of the nuts and put them into a pot, with several inches of water in it- and let them sit overnight (this will leech the colorant out of the husks.) Different numbers of husks may be used for this purpose- the more husks the less the liquid will need to be boiled and simmered.

The next day, boil it for a few minutes to leech remaining colorant, and then let it simmer for a good two hours.

When this has been completed, and the fluid cooled, you ought to remove any husk chunks or particles from the mix- the best way to do this is by straining through a cheesecloth or similar material, but it is possible to do so using a wire mesh as well (which will be left with a large brown stain on it, as I once discovered much to my mothers' dismay years ago.)

The strained material will be too diluted to use as a true ink- it will need to be simmered for perhaps several hours more, until it thickens- you can test the material periodically, simply by dipping your chosen writing implement into the brew and writing a few lines of text- the ink that results is extremely dark brown, and doesn't bleed out into the material much (which is very good.)

Some recipes call for preserving the ink by adding alcohol- normally vodka is used, but I prefer to use a strong gin (which is just as potent and has a nice scent.) Once preserved as such, the ink should technically last forever, although it will settle over time and must be stirred before use- this particular ink, while not as attractive as those made using blackberries or dragon's blood, doesn't seem to fade or run, and is very easy to make. Recipes can be searched for online, although some good books of woodcraft and at-home hobbies may contain much the same material.

Fruits of Eden, Herbalism and the Occult

MAKING BLACKBERRY INK

For the creation of ink from berries (blackberries being the most commonly used and most colorful) it will be necessary to gather a rather large number of berries first and foremost- these ought to be ripe or even slightly past their prime, as unripe berries will not work properly.

Much like with black walnut ink, the berries will stain anything they touch (although berry juice is not nearly as long lasting as walnut stains unless they contact with light colored clothing, it can be a mess to clean up anyways.) Because of this, gloves are preferable although not strictly necessary. Blackberry stains will appear bright purple on white clothing so wear a throw-away shirt and pants if there's any chance of it getting on your light colored fabrics.

Mash the berries into a bowl either with your hands or some other implement- they need to be juiced fairly thoroughly, and subsequently this mash should be heated in a pot with some apple cider or white vinegar added to it as a preservative (about a quarter to half a cup will work fine.) When heated, vinegar releases certain toxic chemicals, and thus this process should be performed with a window open and a fan in it to vent the fumes, although cooking this relatively small amount of vinegar is unlikely to do anything but cause your lungs some mild irritation. (Read: Asthmatics need to be more careful than others with this process.) The cooking can also be done outdoors.

Stir the mash and vinegar mix and let it cook on a low heat for 15 minutes- now let it cool; it is now ready to be strained in a manner similar to the black walnut ink already discussed, with a wire mesh and, preferably, with a cheesecloth which will remove the vast majority of smaller particles and homogenize the ink. Strain it off into a bowl or jar, but be careful because this part of the process is particularly messy.

The ink, thus strained, is essentially ready for use- you can choose to simmer it longer to thicken it slightly, or you can add gum arabic (as some recipes suggest, although I have not tried it myself) which is said to thicken it artificially- it can now be bottled and is ready for use.

Over time the ink tends to darken somewhat, although if it is exposed to light it will eventually fade (unlike walnut ink which seems resistant to fading until used on paper.)

I have heard that raspberries are just as useful, yielding a bright pinkish-red ink. I haven't myself attempted to make this (because I didn't need the color) but most berries seem to create ink, and the recipes for all of them seem roughly similar, with the primary difference being the difficulty mashing and preserving the material depending on how much vinegar needs to be added. Sadly, blueberries do not actually create blue ink, being translucent and green inside, and not true blue.

Between walnut (brown) blackberry (purple) and raspberry (pinkish red) you now have a host of colors for illuminating manuscripts or for creating sigils naturally- this ink is, again, also far cheaper than relying on buying it in large quantities which might be necessary for such work, for which a ballpoint pen will not suffice.

MAKING DRAGON'S BLOOD INK

Of all the natural inks listed here (among many other possible recipes including the most famous involving coprinus mushrooms which is too arcane for me to recreate) dragon's blood's recipe will yield perhaps the most useful ink. Being that the "darker" occult manuscripts often involve the use of red colorant dragon's blood is a must for those practicing the darker paths. Importantly, this ink will stain surfaces almost with the same vigor as black walnut hulls will, so use gloves unless you wish to look like a serial killer.

The first step in this recipe is to simply powder the resin- this can be more easily and quickly achieved by freezing it first, which helps to desiccate (dry) and weaken its molecular structure, so that it can be powdered finely using the same stone mortar and pestle which I have listed before for other purposes. It needs to be *very* finely powdered, and merely mixed with powdered gum arabic (an equal amount to the amount of resin powder you have prepared, roughly) and then the lot of it mixed with alcohol (again, a high-octane gin is my preferred alcohol for all extractions and inks, but vodka or everclear will also work.) You need to add enough alcohol such that the mixture, when stirred, is homogeneous but not runny- add it slowly and stop adding it when the mixture is even and appears liquefied but still slightly sticky (if it is too runny, the mixture will be useless.) I can't give an exact ratio of alcohol to add to the mix, but 10 parts alcohol to each part of resin seems to work properly.

    This ink should now be strained (although it is likely nearly homogeneous) after stirring it for 10 minutes or so to enrich it and leech out any colorant from the powdery mix- you can use a cheesecloth for this purpose, although a simple white cotton cloth will work just as well (the cloth will look like it recently came from a shooting victim with a large blood-red stain so use only cloth you intend to discard or reuse solely for this purpose.)

    The ink is now able to be bottled- even a relatively small amount of it will work just fine for repeated usage, although as before it will not work with most standard pens, thus a calligraphy pen or other pointed stylus will be necessary. Sadly, none of these ink recipes can replace standard printer ink, which costs more by weight than solid, pure gold, or finely cut diamond, and is the most expensive substance in the entire world.

CREATING SMUDGES

    Smudges of dried plant material are a suitable replacement for the somewhat more difficult-to-make incense sticks or cones normally used in ritualism. Certain types of smudges (especially those formed from white sage) are highly prized and commonly used in cleansing rituals and for exorcism purposes, or for healing, or for other purposes (or just to release a great deal of relaxing scent.)

    With any smudges, you will need only a few tools and materials- a type of dried plant material to form the actual base of the smudge, as well as twine or string (preferably of an organic nature- hemp string and regular twine are both dirt cheap and suitable for smudges) and something to shear the plant material to an appropriate length.

    Gather the dried plant material together into a sort of bundle- it should not be extraordinarily compressed and dense, but it cannot be overly loose either- in the former case it will burn improperly, and in the latter case it will fall apart in its twine and potentially cause a fire (as such, smudges should be held over a non-flammable object when burned; a bowl or plate or any metallic or ceramic implement will work, although wooden implements are unlikely to ignite from the small amount of ash and cinder released.)

    The bundle will be uneven- but it should be bound together with twine before it is sheared- wrap the material such that it is compact and "roughly cylindrical" in shape (it will not be perfect) and begin by wrapping the twine around one end, perhaps an inch from one side where you intend to shear it off to even it out- wrap the twine around the smudge in both directions, and then work your way back down to keep it tight, simply tying a knot when the bundle is wrapped- this is not difficult.

    Now that the smudge is bundled, shear off both ends about a half inch to an inch from the edges of the twine- this will allow a small area to begin to smolder and release scent, without accidentally burning the twine apart before the end has itself turned to ash. Most materials suitable for smudges- especially white sage or catnip, are slightly sticky or have "fuzzy" leaves and stems and the materials will bind together slightly, meaning there is little more for the twine to do than keep the regular or semi-regular shape of the smudge itself. When one side of the twine burns the other parts of it will hold the smudge together just as well.

A good smudge should, when squeezed gently, have some give to it (in other words, it shouldn't feel immobile and dense as a brick.) small bits of plant material may or may not flake off of the smudge, but if stored properly in a glass jar or similar safe location it should last for years or decades without decomposing. If stored in a paper towel in a glass jar, a smudge will also keep its scent for a very long time- the paper towel regulates moisture. You can store many smudges in this way.

White sage is the most commonly created type of smudge- its resinous texture and somewhat dexterous leaves and stems make it ideal for such purposes, but catnip and other plants as listed in this book have the same qualities for creating a smudge. White sage is frequently available in co-ops and on the internet in smudge form.

In this age of genetically modified crops it is always good that any material used in what will likely become a healing or spiritually cleansing smudge comes from organically grown plants. The types of herbs grown for this type of use rarely if ever need fertilizer or genetic modifications to grow to fantastic sizes anyways. Catnip will grow on a pile of sand with little else to sustain it.

CREATING PAPER FROM PAPYRUS OR OTHER NATURAL SOURCES

The creation of paper is not all that difficult- the difficulty lies, primarily, in obtaining enough materials to actually create enough of it for commercial use. The reader will likely be using it on a fairly small scale, for which a few sheets of papyrus or even a simple toadstool (which makes a writing surface if not actual paper) will suffice. Paper birch bark can also be used for a completely naturalistic paper- although these tend to flake off over time and are not ideal except for temporary use (IE: as a written invocation that will then be burned as an offering or spell) or as a fun decorative addition to the occultists' arsenal. If your intent is to make birch bark paper the instructions are simple; find some paper birch trees (they are white, with black or dark gray stripes, quite tall and spindly) and find large chunks of the curled, very thin bark below the tree. Do not rip pieces off of the trees themselves- this may cause disease in the living tissues. This is quite literally the entire guide I can give regarding birch bark. You may steam and press it to flatten it, then trim it to size, as well.

    Papyrus is one of the oldest materials used for paper- and while we often think of it being grown in Egypt along the Nile, it is possible for anyone in a temperate climate to grow it- its shoots are reportedly tasty but its main purpose is as a starchy grass or reed which may be lightly processed in order to yield a durable, fairly high quality paper, with a rough surface which makes it quite good for retaining materials painted or written onto it. This papyrus paper can essentially be made indefinitely large in size, or can be cut into appropriate sheet lengths (using a standard piece of paper, for example, as a template for cutting.) If the reader is keeping a sort of dream journal or similar occult text, it is possible to bind papyrus paper in much the same way as any other material, but it will be of better quality than any pulp paper and comparable to hemp paper, which you can see for yourself if you buy any book written before the 1930s.

    Growing the papyrus from seed can be difficult considering the tiny size of the seeds, but a rather small patch of it will work fine- it should achieve a height of five feet or more in a single season on any decent soil assuming it is kept moist- when harvesting the plant the best material (most ideal for paper making) is within three feet or so of the base- the tops can be discarded. These plants may achieve far larger sizes as well. Properly cared for the stalks will grow in a manner not entirely dissimilar to that of the corn plant.

Fruits of Eden, Herbalism and the Occult

Using a knife, remove the outer green layer, exposing the whitish core of the stalk. This must now be cut into thin strips. (Because papyrus is starchy and almost like a layered and flaky wood, this is actually fairly easy as the blade will pierce straight through it following the intricacies of the vein-work within this woody core.)

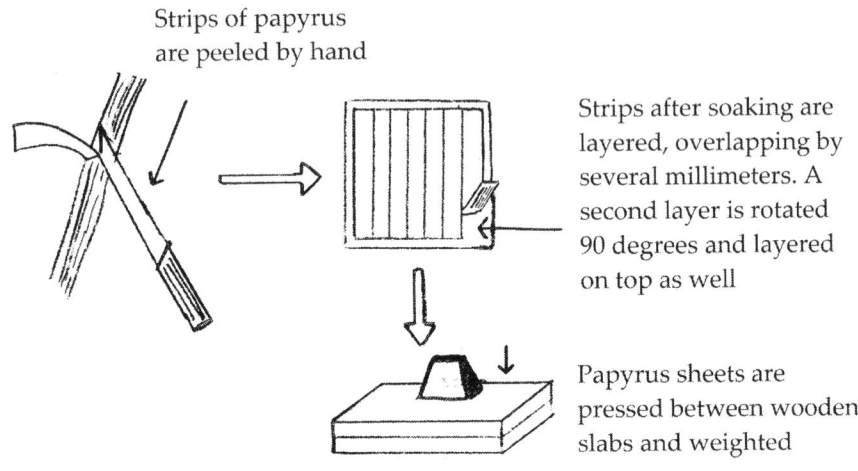

Strips of papyrus are peeled by hand

Strips after soaking are layered, overlapping by several millimeters. A second layer is rotated 90 degrees and layered on top as well

Papyrus sheets are pressed between wooden slabs and weighted

The strips must be soaked in water in order to soften them, although I have seen people simply go right to work pressing the paper, which yields a decent but more easily destroyed paper which comes apart quickly. Place all strips of core into a large basin of warm water and let them sit for at least 24 and no more than 72 hours- adding a small amount of sugar- a few tablespoons- to this mix will improve its quality (something I myself discovered.) Do not worry about trimming them to size yet- you can, but it makes more sense to create the paper and completely process it and then, subsequently, trim it when it is dry and you can be sure about the resultant dimensions of the sheet or sheets you have created.

The strips should now be slightly spongy in texture- they need to be laid out flat to dry partially for perhaps a half hour or so after letting them drip for a few seconds- a wooden surface will help absorb

Fruits of Eden, Herbalism and the Occult

a small amount of the fluid they contain.

    Now, lay the strips lengthwise on a flat surface such that they slightly overlap- it doesn't matter if they are perfectly even but each strip should overlap the next by a few millimeters- this way when pressed, they will bind together. Continue this until you have a sheet that is roughly the desired length or slightly larger.

    Now, lay another layer of papyrus strips in the opposite direction on the first layer, rotated 90 degrees, such that the two layers will overlap completely, so that, when pressed flat and dried, they will bind to one another, substantially increasing durability. This paper will not yet look attractive.

    Traditional recipes call for pounding these sheets before pressing them- you may do so if you wish using a simple flat-bottomed rock or perhaps a brick, but it is possible this will destroy the sheet itself should you do so incorrectly. You may experiment with this method if you believe you have enough material to waste a bit experimenting, otherwise you may press it flat without pounding. The purpose of the pounding is predominantly to crush the materials of the papyrus flesh where each layer overlaps, causing them to bind tightly.

    Now the time consuming aspect comes into play- the sheet should now be left on its flat surface and covered with another flat object upon which a weight is left- in Egypt this would have been, usually, two pieces of wood and a large rock placed on top for up to a week, but if you have the ability to use a system with several vices and a frame this will work even better. Multiple layers can be pressed by alternating layers of papyrus sandwiched in thin layers of wood. A single weight can thus compress many layers of papyrus- a few, a dozen, or a thousand depending on the intricacy of such a system.

    In any case, the sheet or sheets of papyrus strips, pressed between two flat objects and weighted down, will need to be left for approximately a week, somewhat less if you are using a system of vices. I am not sure if plastic can be used for this purpose. I believe that, generally, it's best if the layers used are themselves slightly absorbent (read; made of wood.)

The finished product will be a tan or brownish color, or may be a beige yellow depending on the method of processing- once dry you may cut it to whatever shape you wish. This material is extremely good for use in illumination, evocative sigils, and as stand alone pages for making notes, and at the very least will lend a naturalistic flair to your craft. When people realize you've made your own paper- out of papyrus, no less, it will presumably impress them. These sheets, properly worked, could also be made into literal scrolls to be bound to wooden rods- a thirty foot section would require some time to produce but it can be done.

Conversely, for an extremely simple natural writing surface, you may choose to go into the woods and harvest toadstools- these tree growing, hard-topped mushrooms have a soft, white or off-white underside which can be written on simply by applying pressure, as in with a small stick, pen, or your finger- toadstools are generally nontoxic and as such touching them is highly unlikely to cause harm, however they are also not edible, and will cause vomiting due to their extremely woody texture and foul taste.

Toadstools may be small- a few inches in diameter- or they might be massive, and several feet across. There was a toadstool in my childhood hometown that was at least two feet across and persisted in the same location for the better part of a decade before disappearing, only to be replaced by three or four more toadstools of the same species, each smaller but still impressive in size. When the toadstool dries out it may still be written on, but any pressure at all applied to the soft underside *will* leave a mark. If you drop the toadstool the wrong way, or accidentally press it with your finger, it will be marked by the damage forever.

Care must be taken not to over harvest the toadstools- for

although the active part of the organism is actually inside a decaying chunk of tree, the toadstool itself is essentially a reproductive organ containing spores, and harvesting too many of them can drive the local population into temporary extinction. Sustainable occultism is good occultism.

CHAPTER NINE
Finding or creating an Outdoor Ritual Space

For those choosing to use nature in their ritual work, the creation of a temporary or permanent outdoor location for their rites can be both fulfilling and enjoyable- those who are "energy sensitive" may find themselves naturally finding locations suitable for either positive or negative ritual workings- even those who are not can design an area on their own to emulate their workings.

The creation of an outdoor space solely for the working of rituals can be important, especially within certain crafts and schools of the occult, and may be a fulfilling experience with health benefits, relaxing the occultist during their rites. For its secular purposes alone, the creation of an outdoor space, or multiple spaces, is a good skill to develop, even for those not specifically practicing any path at all.

I will use my own outdoor space as an example- for within my own garden, there is a relatively large area between beds which I myself use for both meditative relaxation and occult workings- it's essentially flat, and roughly eight feet wide and twenty long, supplying more than enough room for, say, the creation of a circle, or the erection of a temporary altar, or any other necessary ritual trappings for magickal work. At times, I use bricks to form a circle and use this rather than a circle made, say, of salt, for utterly natural ritual workings which require little to no preventative protection. Oddly, brick dust has voodoo connotations, although I do not use it as such.

The area is partly shaded by my peach tree- which itself grew almost miraculously because I never planted it there and it apparently sprung up on its own from a pit thrown into the compost pile in years prior. In this shade, surrounded by herbs and flowers of great magickal potency on their own, the energy of rituals is increased by an order of magnitude. It is also a tasty location. What better way to practice than to never have to leave the garden for a snack?

There was a time, in the past, when people were more in tune with nature (they had to, for they lived in nature every day of their lives) and when they could easily tell what areas would be suitable for each type of ritual. For this purpose they erected, using largely materials supplied by nature itself, their altars of wood and stone, their sacred groves, and decorated their sacred caves and tombs with dyes made from plants and also materials derived from animals. Ocher, too, specifically, was of great importance, mined from certain areas and used as body paint and for drawing things in caves.

For the creation of a true outdoor ritual space, the climate must be considered- a cool, wet climate like we have here in New England will not be suitable for the same species of plants, or energetic decorations, as, say, the deserts of the southwestern United States, or the fields and meadows of central Europe. While the person designing the ritual space must take mainly their own personality and desires into consideration, there are a few energetic qualities to consider that seem relatively standard across the variable occult systems, and which seem mostly uniform across populations. An entire study could be made on cross-cultural comparisons of these energies and backgrounds as they relate to magickal rituals, prayer, and religion in general.

CONSIDERING THE BIOME

The general "feel" of an area can be determined partially by the surroundings- a perpetually dark, fog-enshrouded area will likely harbor what most humans would consider a creepy ambiance, while a brightly lit, flower filled meadow is more likely to be seen as positive. These energy values exist within a subjective psychological framework, but part of the occult is aligning ones' emotions with their rituals- and because of this, even though the opinions formulated regarding the positive or negative aspects of a given area will be subjective, it is nonetheless of importance. This is not limited to the occultist designing a garden, but may be a totally natural region where they choose to set up a simple stone altar or merely practice their rites. Since these areas may be located in state parks, on federal land, and in similar scenarios, it is always best to check whether the desired area is owned privately or by some governing body, and if so whether it is legal to both enter the area, and, if it is, to erect any sort of structure (even if it be a flat rock on top of other rocks for a makeshift altar.) Here in New England a lot of forested land is owned by the state or by various towns themselves, but nobody appears to (generally) care if you re-arrange a stack of rocks. That is not to say permission should not be sought to do so, however.

For example, in my own practice, I find that it is in my garden that positive rituals are most easily performed and to a greater effect than elsewhere- and for negative rituals I do not need to travel far, because there are several darker, cooler, more private locations scattered around the forests where these can be performed. The garden itself is too colorful, too "alive" with activity, to perform negative ritualism because it is not possible for me to get into the correct frame of mind to use such ritualism when I am there. It's difficult to lay a death curse in a patch of flowers.

For negative rituals, there are certain regions that seem to excel for such works- dark pine forests are among the best, along with any forested area that is perpetually enshrouded by darkness. This idea might seem like a Hollywood cliche, but if it is psychological energy we are looking for, it doesn't matter if it has been hijacked and perverted into a fictional archetype by abrahamists out to pocket some quick cash releasing yet another slasher flick. Indeed, the collective psychology of a culture is partly determined by the entertainment it ingests- most people will take these fictional cliches as real.

Highlands areas, in the mountains, tend to be dark and cool anyways in any eastern, forested area. Swampy locales are particularly good because they may essentially be dead zones- in drier climates, a plateau or mesa might be crisscrossed with cavern systems, evoking dark energies from deep within the earth, seeping slowly to the surface- and even though they may be sunny and warm, they also may be zones of low or dead energy. In urban zones, energy tends to be denoted by whether a neighborhood is thriving or blighted. Unfortunately, the blighted ones are rather unsafe to be performing rituals in.

Any area connected with noted or widely regarded paranormal phenomena automatically assumes a sort of negative energy form regardless of whether these phenomena are real. I am of the theoretical school that believes that the paranormal, regardless of whether it is genuinely *real* is at least real in a *de facto* sense because the mass psychological effect of people merely believing it to be true is capable of altering the energetic flow in the region. For example, an abandoned building may be rumored through urban legend to be abandoned because it is haunted by the lingering spirit of a psychotic spree killer. Even if the story itself is false, the area will still begin to stagnate through the collective will of those who believe it. People will go there, get spooked, impregnate it with feelings of fear or apprehension, and continuously pump the area with their own ghastly thought forms.

In cases where the urban legend (true or false) involves circulation among a younger audience, the effects are even greater. Children (and adults who retain childlike fascination with the paranormal, "scary", and generally morbid) as well as the psychologically maladjusted, exude a far more potent effect on their surroundings than even most practicing adult occultists. If the forest is said to be haunted by the local children, be assured the energy there is stagnant, perhaps even outright malevolent. The perfect location to practice negative rituals, which will amplify, direct, and absorb these negative currents. In a hilarious twist of fate, the collective belief of any randomly sampled group of middle schoolers that a place in the woods is "haunted" will eventually, in time, attract occultists or spirits of some kind, and their belief is thus caused to be *very real.* Plenty of secular individuals will scoff at the idea- I invite them to study theoretical physics and string theory and get back to me.

People living in some parts of the world are more blessed than others when it comes to accessing negative energy for their rituals- these may be in urban zones (although in many cases it is illegal or at least dangerous to access abandoned buildings like sanitariums and old prisons) or rural areas, such as the barren rocky lands of Scotland, the fjords in Scandinavia, certain ancient ruins in the middle east- all across the world are scattered locations of extreme occult power. I have often wondered what the result would be should a large enough gathering of occultists converge on the Pantheon in Athens or the Great Pyramid in Egypt and begin chanting their incantations; the effect would be, at least to them, quite profound I am sure. Perhaps it behooves me to recommend, though, the oracle chamber of the Hypogeum at Malta instead for such a future mass rite.

Warmer climates seem to have fewer zones of negativity (perhaps because of all the fun in the sun they have.) This isn't universally the case however, as one of the most potent zones of negative energy in the world is the Bermuda Triangle. This area is largely ocean and thus can't be used for rituals (unless you own a ship) but it does contain certain islands or pieces of them, which are themselves quite beautiful but which lay on an apparent magnetic anomaly which funnels deep energies to the surface. (An entire book could be written on the subject of this area as it relates to occult energies- perhaps a project for the future, or some other gifted occultist.) I've been to Florida and despite the happy, shining beaches, there are also a lot of dark, swampy spots near Tampa Bay. Unfortunately, the risk of being attacked by an alligator, constrictor, or wild boar is high enough to make them a bit more dodgy than the forests of New England, cold as they may sometimes be.

The ancients seemed to understand the manipulation of energetic zones for occult workings- all across the world there are outcroppings of stones which have been erected seemingly with the purpose to drive magnetic lines across them. (The stones themselves being magnetic, often quarried from inordinate distances when other stone was available locally.) When you see the pyramids, Stonehenge, or perhaps even the Bimini Road, (now submerged in the sea) you are seeing structures that appear to have been built with some understanding of magnetism and energy. And while the occultist is unlikely to be able to erect a megalith, a much smaller project of similar style can be made and used to the same effect.

A zone of negative energy can also be artificially created (while still being essentially natural in format) as well. Simply planting a shady grove of spruce and placing an elongated stone upright in the center of it, surrounded by some berry bushes, nightshade, and so forth, might be enough for such workings. It is not particularly difficult to create these artificial dead zones, should no natural ones be available- however they are so prevalent even in the most happy of regions that this is probably not necessary to do. The species present in an area have an effect upon the energy available. Behind my home there was once a rather large area of small, dense pine, with a pair of fairly narrow paths, which were always quiet, dark, and filled with mushrooms and ferns because of the pine growth around the area. It was dark, and comforting even if a bit creepy. Now that the area is cleared, the energy is more neutral. It was briefly a meadow of sorts full of wildflowers with a few sumac trees and was positive in its value. It is not always the location but rather its content that matters- here is another secret; mythology relating an area as positive or negative is often spawned because of its appearance, including the life forms generally inhabiting it. This directly informs a great deal of mans' mythology and legend.

In the case of positive energy it is just as easy to obtain a location that can be useful for your rites or rituals- it is far easier (and cheaper) to create a positive zone. Even a small garden, if planted over with flowers and herbs, forms a small "bubble" of life energy- this is in part due to the sexual symbolism involved with most flowering species- the sacred feminine, the very essence of the left hand path, is an important aspect to disorderly (but usually positive) energy movement- were it not for perturbations and chaos the entire universe would be stagnant- and it is in blood that birth itself happens. There is a reason why flowers are traditionally likened to the feminine.

While the garden is a potent energetic zone, any meadow or grove of deciduous growth tends to harbor positive energy- farmlands, whether old and fallow or new and active, function in a similar manner. Any individual will harbor slightly different opinions on what constitutes a zone of happy, positive, active, or "nice" energy.

A mountainous meadow of beauty and life may be bordered on all sides by a ring of literal death- perhaps a dark, deathly silent forest which hasn't seen an ax in centuries. The earth's life force operates upon the exact same principles as the solar cycle of sunspots and coronal holes- in order for the maximum energy to be achieved, the zones have to be in proximity, and interact with one another. There is a low for every high and a good for every bad (at least where we regard the subjective dichotomy at all.) Most of the more scary paranormal stories ever crafted by those who began exploring, settling, and expanding into the new world, took place not in areas already settled but in the wilderness bordering human settlement. In other cases, paranormal tales from settled areas typically involved either small communities on the margins of larger ones (Salem notably so) or outcasts and those on the margins of a larger society (spinsters, widows, those living in the outer, generally more poor regions of settled land.) Early tales from the new world wilderness often came from hunters, trappers, and explorers, unless they were directly adapted from Native lore. For an excellent analysis of this as it relates to (mostly) aquatic cryptids and mythology surrounding them, I highly recommend Michel Meurger and Claude Gagnon's excellent work *Lake Monster Traditions; a Cross Cultural Analysis*. There is no better work on the subject, at least that I have ever encountered.

And as to the subject of the Hollywood cliche upon such locations, such imagery is primarily used *because* it affects the human population, which is innately fine tuned to understand these energies, through sensory abilities that science has not yet quantified properly, as some claim perhaps related to the pineal gland or some other mental function of little study. Finding a positive area to perform positive rituals might be as simple as finding a patch of flowers growing next to a small river flowing down the side of a mountain. When we regard the historical occult we generally can only understand it through human remains; ruins, which have not deteriorated with time. If natural spaces untarnished by megaliths, burials, and so forth, were used for rituals in any culture, we often cannot know it to be the case with any certainty, unless tools and other materials were left behind from the same.

Minerals have always been a part of the occult world, from alchemy to high or ritual magick, to even the most physical school of modern day Wicca.

Quartz is perhaps the most regarded of minerals for absorbing, dispelling, and directing energy- particularly in the case of energies that are positive. Any area containing outcroppings of white quartz, amethyst (purple quartz) or rose quartz (which is pink) are generally seen as positive. It seems that there is a traditional view to seeing crystals as mostly positive and sedimentary stone as negative or stagnant but neutral in energy value. Sharp crags of slate appear a bit more foreboding to the average person, it seems, than a sparkling pile of smoky quartz.

The physical, particularly geometric qualities of minerals (and perhaps other materials) seem to be a constant theme in some occult traditions as well; this can be used to the advantage of the occultist in identifying or altering an area to perform rituals within. You could, in theory, create a gigantic, continuous bordered garden in the shape of a thirty foot wide pentagram, and then throw chunks of quartz into it, erecting a gigantic crystal right in the center- and while your neighbors would be livid, it would indeed create a good ritual space. The only drawback to such a working, if you feel indeed that it is appropriate to make such a space, is the risk of those external to yourself worrying that you may be afflicted with lunacy of some sort or another.

Fruits of Eden, Herbalism and the Occult

Sacred geometry is not particularly necessary when working with outdoor spaces- you can (if you have studied the subject) include it in your work, but these trappings are more for those who have the time and cash necessary to do a greater deal of work. I have found that it is more important to select the species carefully which will be cultivated, than to obsess over design.

If your ritual space is within the confines of your property, then it makes sense to build your garden around this area. You may choose, as I have, to keep a central location open, and place beds around it on some or all sides, so that you can provide both a screen for privacy (with hedges, sunflowers, corn rows, or any other taller plant) as well as ready access to herbs you may wish to use in your rituals. I have experimented (but have had little success) with building rounded beds, but that was far in the past when I didn't fully understand the process of composting, and I fear I killed my plants with improperly created compost at that time.

The use of wood and stone in the garden doesn't just create a natural ritual space, it also beautifies it- it is possible using a trellis to create an almost tunnel-like system in which the entire area is semi-enclosed by vines and other plants- some plants will grow on stone, stretching vines across it and engulfing them (particularly morning glory plants, which are listed in the psychoactive section.) If the path between your beds is a yard wide, or thereabouts, you could create an enclosed path using little more than some stakes which have had rods conjoined to them, to cover the top of the path. Any swiftly-growing annuals capable of climbing a trellis can then be planted at the base of such a system.

If you live in a northern climate like I do, you must keep in mind that during the winter months most or all of your garden plants will be dead, and those that are not will likely be in hibernation. Very few plants retain any sort of vitality below freezing; for this purpose, if you did erect any sort of system to bring privacy to your ritual area, you can still retain this privacy; if, for example, you grew layers of corn to surround your ritual space, simply disregard cutting the brush down and let it stand over winter- the cold and wind will slowly degrade the stalks, leaving only chunks of stalk near the base perhaps a foot or two tall, but for most of the winter the area will remain screened- hedges are a better choice, as they are generally evergreens, remaining fully awake and alive during cold weather.

The creation of your ritual space does not need to be complicated- it can be simple, a few small beds with a flat rock, if you choose to opt for the more easy path. You can make it as large as you have space for or desire- my own garden is quite large in size, but because I also grow edible crops and herbs meant for the kitchen, less of my room is reserved for mystically useful purposes; however, the aesthetics of the area are very good. I deliberately designed it with both function and beauty in mind.

The best time for fertility rituals, and rituals related to love or lust, is in the spring (in climates that are cooler) or in the usually more wet winters in warmer climates- most ritualistic schools of thought give particular importance to the spring and fall equinox, as well as to both solstices- the spring equinox is a great time for major rites to be worked.

Again, as to the theory of psychological energy, regardless of what ritual space you happen to be using, periods of the year seen by the average person as creepy or frightening can be useful for curses and other negative ritualism. Halloween (or Samhain) comes to mind (even though the modern holiday is more about candy than evil spirits to the average child.) You may choose to do some light research concerning urban legends and myths in your general area, and create rituals designed around dates of importance you may stumble upon- and it is likely there will be many. It is important for me to briefly mention here that I am well aware that Samhain, in its authentic sense, is a positive and not negative or "creepy" celebration- but it is seen as such by much of western culture nonetheless.

You may also choose to simply move rituals indoors when weather is not particularly fit for working them- for this purpose you might choose to dedicate a room to these works within your home or apartment- perhaps decorating it with various potted herbs and other plants- I have not created a dedicated indoor space for my own work, although I do keep a large number of potted plants in the bedroom for my own amusement.

The important thing to remember, when crafting a ritual space either in or outdoors, is to create a setup which works *for you* and you may very well realize that your own style of decoration differs from those of others, including my own recommendations. To you, a dark, sedate forest of dying pine may have a positive vibe to it- a sort of relaxing quality that completely reverses its meaning. In these cases, this is not a defect of any kind, merely your own psychology recognizing these same energies as positive, which others may find threatening.

CHAPTER TEN
Index of plants of occult importance

An exhaustive list of plants and a short description of their use within occultism- the design of this book precluded the addition of many hundreds of plants and fungi which are used for such purposes, but for which either insufficient historical context is known, or where use is solely modern, or dubious. Some herbs here were also precluded due to the extreme number of pages which would have been necessary to include all plants and fungi in the encyclopedic entries within this work.

INDEX OF SPECIES

Allspice: Sometimes added to satchels and other charms to promote wealth.

Almond: Used to promote wealth- may be added to incense as an extraction. Edible, with a pleasant scent.

Aloe: Medicinally used to treat burns, also kept as a stand-alone charm as decoration for prosperity.

Alyssum: Burned or used as a charm in order to dispel negativity and create peace.

Amaranth: Amaranth seed and dried plant parts are used in potpourri, and the plant itself is grown in order to encourage peace and prosperity.

Fruits of Eden, Herbalism and the Occult

Anise: Used medicinally, or to protect the bearer.

Ash: Carved into altars or other occult implements- may also be burned for ritual fires.

Aster: Used in potpourri or other forms while working love related magick. May be grown in a garden for similar purposes.

Avocado: Sometimes carved with symbols and used in spells to increase physical attractiveness, or secure love.

Balm of Gilead: Considered both protective and psychically cleansing when grown or kept in proximity.

Bamboo: Commonly grown (or dried and collected) and kept in a household for good luck. Its shoots are edible.

Barley: Collected in a sheaf and kept around the house for luck and wealth (and commonly used as such by new age groups- my mother kept several sheaves of barley on the wall for this reason.)

Basil: Considered protective when kept in a satchel or under a pillow.

Bay (laurel): Worn or otherwise used to secure and perpetuate victory and protection of material wealth.

Birch (paper birch): Sometimes the bark is inscribed with invocations or the wood burned for protection- this may have some origin in the use of Amanita mushrooms which favor paper birch as a parasitic host for their hyphae. Paper birch is excellent for any fires made, as it will burn almost as well when wet and green as it will when dried, due to its papery flesh.

Blackberry: Both the fruit and dried vines are used in rituals to protect the individual and bring them prosperity- the vines may be burned in ritual flame. Thorns should be sanded off before the vines are handled by children.

Bleeding Heart: Normally grown or kept in proximity to secure love. The heart-shaped flowers may be added to a satchel, potpourri, or used in other rituals (particularly image rituals) to secure love.

Blue Cohosh: Considered a health-promoting plant. Part of an abortifacient brew used since ancient times which also contains pennyroyal and may be paired with a parsley pessary administered vaginally.

Blue Lotus: Hypnotic-sedative used to encourage visions and lucid dreams. Use dates to ancient Egypt and Greece.

Boneset: Sometimes used in folk medicine for exorcism purposes.

Bundleflower: A plant containing DMT important in modern ayahuasca rituals or as a source of purified DMT itself.

Burdock: A highly medicinally active plant whose roots may be kept in dried form for protection against spirits or negativity.

Calamus: Used in satchels or in potpourri to encourage the flow of wealth.

Caraway: A fragrant herb species whose vapors are used in extracted incense or in raw form to encourage psychic visions, or to allow remote viewing.

Catnip: A potently fragrant mint plant which is used in love spells, normally in the form of a satchel. This ritualism might be related to its effect upon cats (and/or the relation of cats to feminine, sexual energy.)

Fruits of Eden, Herbalism and the Occult

Cat Tail: A large plant which produces an abundance of brown pod-like seeding bodies in swampy areas. The unripe seeding shafts are dried and kept around to promote lust and to regain or maintain sexual function and drive. They are supposedly edible as well.

Cedar: A type of wood commonly burned to purify and cleanse an area and prevent negative energy from entering the region. Chunks of dried cedar wood are very fragrant and used as mulch.

Chamomile: Medicinally used to encourage sleep, and spiritually used as a scent to remove evil intent. Both the German and Roman types are edible.

Chicory: The root has been used as herbal tea for centuries- and the flowers or root (or both) may be dried and used to quiet lust.

Chrysanthemum: Dried and kept in satchels or in a home to protect the occupants from harm.

Citron: Potently fragrant, the plant is kept in proximity to stave off disease and to encourage psychic visions.

Clove: Used in folk remedies for driving out evil spirits and protecting homes.

Clover: Famously used to encourage and retain good luck, particularly with regards to preventing injury and illness as well as creating wealth.

Club Moss: Sometimes viewed as good for absorbing and dispelling negative energy by keeping chunks of dried moss in proximity, or allowing it to grow near a home.

Columbine: An attractive flower native to high altitude, sub-alpine environments, it is sometimes dried and kept in the home to promote love.

Fruits of Eden, Herbalism and the Occult

Coriander: Kept in a satchel or under the pillow to retain good health and fortune and for protective reasons. It is also commonly used in edible recipes as a spice.

Corn: Dried as a cob or a whole stalk and used to decorate homes- the more ancient use revolves around ensuring good fortune and harvest, while in modern times it may also be seen as protective.

Crocus: Kept near the bed as a loose potpourri and used to induce vivid dreams or psychic visions.

Cucumber: Grown or used to promote good health in rituals; also famously used in Japan to ward off certain water-dwelling spirits (such as the kappa) by carving one's name in it and throwing it into supposedly haunted waters.

Cumin: Used as one of many herbs in folk remedies for demonic possession through burning or scattering the substance.

Curry: Used to promote wealth and to protect the user. May be used in a manner similar to salt.

Daffodil: The bulbs of this plant are used in various love related spells and, as they bloom quite early in the season, the use may be tied to seasonal cycles.

Datura: A potent hallucinogen-deliriant used to communicate with spirits. The dried pods are additionally said to be useful in blocking hexes by placing them around one's home.

Devil's Shoestring: A type of viburnum- the plant is used in hoodoo ritualism to protect, and the plants are grown around homes to "trip the devil" and keep him from entering.

Dittany (false): Used in curses, where its acrid burning flame is used to burn images of an enemy. It may have been used in necromantic rituals dating to ancient times. Probably the real-life source of the burning bush tale from the bible.

Dogbane: Used in folk medicine, and also within the occult to promote love between partners.

Dragon's Blood: Very commonly used in incense, this fragrant plant is most often used during rituals to protect a spell-caster or a given area.

Ebony: A type of wood commonly used to create altars and wands- its presence is said to encourage increases in the bearer's own power.

Eggplant: Used in curses, particularly during image magic, where it can be inscribed upon.

Eucalyptus: Used in a manner similar to white sage to purify an area with its scent, or to protect a home or person from harm or damage.

Fennel: Used in protective magic when grown within a home's territory. It is claimed that when dew is collected from the leaves of fennel plants (in some American folklore) and used as eye drops, it prevents the deterioration of eyesight.

Feverfew: the flowering parts of this plant are dried and kept in a satchel or potpourri to prevent harm.

Fig: Fig leaves and fruiting bodies are used as decoration within rituals to promote fertility (usage which dates to ancient times in the Mediterranean region.)

Fleabane: Used in dried form to perform exorcisms within folk magick.

Fruits of Eden, Herbalism and the Occult

Frankincense: Often used as incense in various forms, the scent of which is supposed to both exorcise spirits, and to increase the spirituality of those who smell it.

Fumitory: A distant relative of the more commonly known oriental and opium poppies, this plant is used as incense to exorcise demons and has since ancient Greek times. It was commonly used medicinally during the Renaissance.

Garlic: This plant has an extremely long history and scope of use, considered a surefire way to ward off demons and vampires, to retain sexual function, to protect a bearer against harm, and to make a person more physically attractive and youthful- its use spread throughout most of Europe for these purposes and then into the Americas and elsewhere. It is commonly added to food, and regular consumption of garlic is said to ward off parasites, mosquitoes, and fleas.

Ginseng: Used medicinally in Asia, commonly in the form of tea or infusion. It is said to enhance fertility and sexual potency, as well as to retain youth and vigor.

Gourd: Often dried and carved into bowls or cups, gourds are also dried and used as decoration to ward off evil. Gourds can be grown to provide ritual objects for the altar.

Hawaiian Baby Woodrose: A tropical vine bearing psychedelic seeds containing LSA and ergine. Like other ergine and LSA containing seeds (morning glory and snake vine) they are commonly consumed during rituals to partake in the divine, in central America and Mexico.

Hazel (witch hazel): The wood of this tree is most often used for creating wands, although it also has medicinal properties as an astringent.

Hellebore: Sometimes used in curse work, possibly because of its highly poisonous nature.

Henbane: A potent deliriant which is one of several candidates for use as flying ointment among medieval "witches." Its use to communicate with other realms is more authentically occult.

Horehound: Commonly used as an ingredient in candy or food, horehound is also used in ritual format to protect health or vitality. Taken as an infusion it is used to prevent or ameliorate sore throats and congestion in folk medicine.

Horseradish: The extremely powerful scent of horseradish is said to repel negative energies and protect the home (possibly because the acrid, burning scent repels animals.) It is also used in a variety of Appalachian foods, and as an additive to many cheese or cream based dips.

Hyssop: Commonly used to purify the home. A ritual bath can be drawn using its materials.

Indian Paintbrush: A common plant which tends to colonize people's lawns- the flowers are kept fresh and around the home to encourage new love, or may be added to a satchel. It spreads as a wildflower.

Irish Moss: Sometimes grown around homes to bring (amusingly) the luck of the Irish to the family therein.

Jasmine: Jasmine is very frequently added to incense (and sometimes scented candles) for its protective powers. There is a similar-smelling but unrelated species of nicotiana called "night scented jasmine" or "jasmine tobacco" which has similar uses and an even more potent scent.

Juniper: Juniper is considered a potent symbol of health, and is sometimes used in incense or potpourri, and has been used in medicine as an antiseptic, which is burned in the home to prevent illness. The Swiss famously had some of the lowest-mortality hospitals of the Renaissance period, and frequently burned juniper, the smoke of which seems to have prevented soldiers' wounds from festering.

Kava: Commonly used as a medicinal mood enhancer, kava is also indicated in rituals designed to increase psychic visions (possibly due to its mildly mind altering nature.)

Larkspur: Larkspur is considered protective in nature and may be grown near and around a home to protect it from burglary or fire.

Lavender: In addition to scenting incense and candles for sleep related purposes, lavender has also been used in a similar manner to protect homes.

Leek: Sometimes grown or eaten for protective purposes- it is considered medicinal in the east. They may be used as a type of wand as well, for various purposes.

Lemon Balm: Lemon balm is used frequently in a medicinal manner to prevent bug bites and parasites such as fleas. It is also applied topically as a general way of protecting the wearer, and may be grown to protect a building.

Licorice: Licorice root is commonly used to protect and create sexual prowess, and the scent is considered to enhance virility and physical health.

Lilac: Most often lilac flowers are kept as an intense and fragrant potpourri thought to preserve physical beauty.

Lotus: The lotus flower (and lotus scent used in incense) is thought to relax an environment, adding positive energy and encouraging the regulation of chaotic cycles.

Fruits of Eden, Herbalism and the Occult

Mallow: The colorful flowering parts of the mallow plant are sometimes used in a potpourri to secure friendship or romance.

Mandrake: While toxic (and a deliriant) mandrake is sometimes kept as a sort of charm. The root often splits to resemble a human form with arms, legs, and a head, and has been used for occult purposes since ancient times. It is thought to protect and promote fertility and health, but it is also used to promote and preserve material wealth.

Marigold: Marigold flowers are often added to autumn decorations in a ritual attempt to prevent sickness and death- the flowers also serve as a deterrent to certain animal pests when planted around the fringes of a garden. Strangely, in Mexican culture, marigold represents death itself.

Mimosa: Probably because some species contain DMT, mimosa is thought to encourage prophetic powers. Some species are inert.

Mistletoe: Mistletoe (famously in Christmas decorations) is used to secure love- the tradition of kissing under the mistletoe probably dates back further, to its use in shamanism.

Morning Glory: Morning glory has a long history of use dating back at least as far as Central American pagan ritualism, containing several psychedelic alkaloids, and used for both prophetic and psychic purposes.

Mullein: Mullein is an exceptionally tall plant with "fuzzy" leaves- and the entire plant is sometimes used as a dried decoration in a manner not unlike the use of stalks and cobs of corn to protect a home. The plant is further used in Native American remedies for asthma when smoked (which may or may not be effective.) Wands made from the dried and sanded stalk are more durable and attractive than most.

Myrrh: A highly protective scent agent, myrrh is also used for exorcisms.

Nettle: Nettles are thought to be medicinal (some sufferers of arthritis use it to restore joint function) and are sometimes boiled and consumed (which is safe when done properly) to restore sexual function in folk remedies.

Olive: Olive branches as decoration, or olive fruit consumption, are thought to enhance fertility.

Onion: Certain types of particularly spicy yellow onions are used in folk medicine from the Mediterranean basin to enhance virility.

Opium Poppy: Opium poppies contain a slew of alkaloids which block pain, but also seem to have some history of being used by occultists for inspiration and to experience enhanced mental prowess over time. A very mild (and unrefined) dose of opium pod sap is perhaps as strong as a few tokes on a marijuana joint.

Pansy: Pansies have been used to secure love in folk magick for many years- they are also grown as a protective agent.

Papyrus: Papyrus stalks seem to have been used in much the same way as corn was in the Americas to protect buildings- the plant is able to be grown in rich soil even in cooler climates, and is also useful for making paper, which may be used to create sigils or stationary. The young shoots are edible.

Parsley: Parsley (which medieval christians warned against using because "its roots grew into Hell") was sometimes used to help induce miscarriage in medieval times by forming it into a pessary and inserting it vaginally, which loosens the cervix. Paired with pennyroyal or blue cohosh tea, or both, it appears to have worked more often than not. It is considered protective in nature, preserving health and youth. Parsley is toxic in large quantities and generally ingested only as a garnish.

Fruits of Eden, Herbalism and the Occult

Passionflower: The passionflower fruit is edible and consumed on its own or in a variety of foods, while its compounds are extracted as a sleep aid. Within the occult realm, both the fruit and herbal supplements extracted from it are used to enhance dream clarity and enter a state of lucid dreaming.

Pennyroyal: Part of the blue cohosh, parsley, pennyroyal trifecta, containing compounds which led to its use at inducing miscarriage. It is grown additionally as a protective, health-increasing herb, and is sometimes ingested as a tea for other medicinal reasons. Tea from this plant is sometimes used for a variety of intestinal complaints.

Pine: Various species of pines are used for good luck and protection- of course including the ancient pagan ritual of hanging trees upside down for solstice celebrations.

Plum: In addition to being a healthy fruit, plums are sometimes used to promote health within rituals- the wood from plum trees has a sweet fragrance and may be added to ritual flame.

Primrose: Primrose is sometimes grown in magick gardens for the sole purpose of protecting the occultist from danger.

Purslane: Purslane is a common weed which grows in gardens on its own across much of the North American continent. It is an extremely healthy plant which may be eaten raw or cooked, and is thought to promote sleep and health when consumed.

Radish: Radishes are sometimes used in folk magick to create lust and romance- the plant may have an incantation said over it and then be left on the property of the person to be affected, or may be collected and kept in one's home to make them attractive to others, or it may be used in image magick.

Fruits of Eden, Herbalism and the Occult

Rose: Roses are an almost universal symbol of love- with the mere presentation of roses often enough to encourage romantic feelings. They are grown, dried, used for decoration, and exchanged for this purpose.

Rosemary: Rosemary is used in incense and potpourri, or kept or grown, to discourage danger or attack, and to protect the bearer of such items.

Rowan: Rowan is grown and used in ritual form to protect and promote health- boughs may be used as decoration for the same goal.

Saffron: Saffron is a rather expensive herb, used for culinary purposes, but equally said to be useful to promote health, vigor, and vitality.

Sage (white): Commonly used for exorcism or for purifying an area- a smudge made from the dried herb may be smoldered, creating a very thick cloud of fragrant smoke. It is also often made into incense, grown outdoors, or used in potpourri

Saint John's Wort: Used in herbal medicine since ancient times, also used to promote health and vitality when ingested or used in ritual. A common feature of many occult gardens. It is frequently used today by women experiencing menopause.

Salvia Divinorum: A replacement for mescal beans in certain North American native rituals, it is a potent hallucinogen and said to take the user to the astral or spirit world- its use dates back for many centuries, but it has been recently re-popularized due to hype on the internet and due to its originally legal status.

San Pedro: A mescaline-containing cactus sometimes used as a replacement for peyote buttons, and used just as frequently in occultism among native peoples, usually strained in boiling water to create a sour tasting "cactus juice"- it is also grown for landscaping purposes.

Sandalwood: Most commonly, sandalwood is used in incense (some incense uses sandalwood as the base around which other fragrances are added within the matrix of the charcoal.) It is used primarily for purification rituals.

Sassafras: Sassafras is most often used as a fragrance to promote health. It appears quite frequently in folk medicine from North America.

Sesame: Sesame seeds and oil are used in fire based rituals in order to release lustful spirits either on the caster or another person, or to protect sexual function or to gain sexual drive. It is considered a very "hot" material within Eastern medicine and mysticism, invigorating and activating the user.

Slippery Elm: Wood from this rather elegant tree is sometimes used to create wands or other occult implements- and is also carved into certain charms (amulets) in order to prevent gossip, the evil eye, or other negative attention from others.

Solomon's Seal: A medicinally active plant used in the East- the plant is used to promote general health, and is sometimes boiled and eaten (and is apparently fully edible.)

Spearmint: Spearmint has been used in North American folk magick for some time, as both a healing herb and one said to increase mental function, including lucid dreaming and astral projection, through its potent fragrance.

Spiderwort: This strange little plant has recently been determined to soak up localized radiation and change color- leading to its use around nuclear power plants- but it's occult purpose is related to obtaining love- and may be added to a satchel or grown for this purpose.

Fruits of Eden, Herbalism and the Occult

Sunflower: Sunflower petals are often added to potpourri, while sunflower oil is sometimes added to ritual flame. Additionally, sunflower seeds are used in folk magick, all of the above being with regards to retaining good health (although different folk rituals involve using the seeds to obtain love as well.)

Sweet Anne: A type of wormwood along with *Absinthium* and *Vulgaris*. Its fragrance is exceptionally strong and may be used in the absence of incense. It can cause itching in some individuals when it is touched, as the flesh of the plant contains volatile oils. The fragrance is vaguely similar to licorice or anise and generally considered pleasant. It will spread wildly and needs to be well controlled.

Tamarind: Tamarind wood is sometimes used to create occult implements such as wands or altars- these implements are considered best for positive or white magick. The fruiting pods are edible in most species and may have significant medicinal and health benefits.

Tea: Tea has among the longest histories of medicinal use of any plant- it is also potently medicinal, and useful in occult poultices and satchels- sometimes to amplify other substances, and sometimes on its own as a fragrance to attract wealth.

Thistle: Thistle flowers are extremely ornate and dried and used as decoration in a manner similar to corn stalks or gourds to protect the health of a family that resides in the decorated area- the roots have been used in folk magick to break hexes.

Thistle (milk): Milk thistle excretes a potent sap which is implicated in protecting the liver from poisons as a purgative. Folk magick indicates that consuming the sap protects an individual from being bitten by snakes.

Thyme: Thyme is one of many herbs thought to increase health when consumed- it is also fragrant and used in satchels.

Fruits of Eden, Herbalism and the Occult

Toadstools: Toadstools are linked to black magick both because of their supposed relation to toads or frogs, and because the underside of a dried toadstool may be used to inscribe the name of a person to be cursed, after which it is anointed upon the altar or burned in ritual flame.

Tobacco (night scented jasmine): A fragrant nicotiana variant which is grown in order to release its potent fragrance in late afternoons and into the night, when the bright flowers bloom. Often placed in occult gardens to attract spirits, repel negativity, or encourage prosperity in one's love life.

Valerian: A commonly used herbal sleep aid- the root has been used to produce a sedating tea for centuries. It is also used to induce romance when two individuals partake of it at the same time, while valerian roots may be used as charms.

Vetch: The large vines of vetch plants may be used in a sort of image magick ritual wherein the names of the occultist and their loved one are bound together with vetch, preventing infidelity.

Violet: Violets are thought to be protective when planted near a home, added to a potpourri or satchel, or when dried and stored. They are used in the same ways to create and retain love or money.

Wild Lettuce: Wild lettuce (or opium lettuce) is often used as a substitute for cannabis, and has various medicinal and occult uses. It is persistent and wild, and quickly dominates marginal areas only to in turn die out locally when soil disturbance ends.

Willow: Willow is medicinal, producing compounds including aspirin- the wood is often used for wands, and dowsing rods, as well as for other divinatory purposes.

Wolfsbane: A powerful deliriant and extremely toxic plant- it is used in curse work, and is inseparably linked both by name and use with anything involving wolves, including the general notion of wolves or anything related to them. This includes metaphors and symbols for predation, madness, and power, as well as lycanthropy. The wiccan's rede mentions this plant, also.

Wormwood (Absinthium): Artemisia Absinthium is the flavoring agent and psychedelic source within absinthe, the "Green Fairy" that so troubled Victorian Europe. The compounds it contains are related to the occult mainly through the ingestion of such liquors by occult authors and practitioners who then produced material for others to consume.

Wormwood (Common): Common wormwood is used frequently in protective magick, especially when added to a satchel, although it is also grown to attract spirits to an area.

Yarrow: Yarrow is most often used in love magick- where it is given to a person after incantations are said, in an effort to bind them to the occultist.

Yew: Yew is an important wood in black magick- with most of its relation to necromancy (both in calling forth spirits by using a yew wand or other yew implements, or physical necromancy in which the toxins it produces are used in a brew for zombification purposes.)

Made in the USA
Lexington, KY
29 December 2017